THE RAW PEARL
was orginally published by Harcourt, Brace & World, Inc.

PEARL BAILEY

The Raw
Pearl

A POCKET BOOK EDITION published by
Simon & Schuster of Canada, Ltd. • Richmond Hill, Ontario, Canada
Registered User of the Trademark

THE RAW PEARL

Harcourt, Brace & World edition published September, 1968

A *Pocket Book* edition

1st printing............July, 1969
2nd printing............July, 1969

This *Pocket Book* edition includes every word
contained in the original, higher-priced edition. It is printed from
brand-new plates made from completely reset, clear, easy-to-read type.
Trademarks registered in the United States and other countries.

Standard Book Number: 671-77084-5.
Library of Congress Catalog Card Number: 67-11963.
Copyright, ©, 1968, by Pearl Bailey. All rights reserved. This *Pocket Book*
edition is published by arrangement with Harcourt, Brace & World, Inc.
Printed in Canada

This book is dedicated to my husband, Louis Bellson—

You, my dear, are the sweet, the warm and beautiful—
Ever busy, ever conscious of your love and responsibility
to your family and friends.
God smiles and touches your face, ever so lightly,
Lifts the corners of your mouth, and hardened hearts melt.
He dips down into his bucket of sunshine and sprinkles
it all over you.
He massages your heart with his hands and brings it to
a burning flame of love for everyone—
You, You, You creature of God—You.

Written in Apple Valley
November 23, 1960
Eight years married

Most autobiographical books by people whom we frequently refer to as celebrities, including actors, entertainers, etc., are either actually written by someone else, though attributed to the celebrity, or are published "as told to" someone else.

This is not the case with Pearl Bailey's book. Another editor, Wendell Shackelford (who worked on the book prior to coming to Harcourt, Brace & World as an editor), and I have worked editorially from the transcript of many tape-recorded conversations with Miss Bailey. We have been at some pains in helping to give the book its final shape to retain not only her own words but, as we think of it, her distinctive voice. We hope that the legion of her admirers will find that voice to be the same in this book as it is when she talks to an audience—vivid, spontaneous, and natural.

—*Hiram Haydn*

There are so many thanks and credits due on *The Raw Pearl*. Let's start with God, who gave me whatever I have.

May I now add my thanks to Mr. Hiram Haydn, who talked me out of my philosophy book and into this one. (Hope it's worth it.) Thanks to the ones who sat through some sessions as I read passages—Peetney, Marie, Louie, Mickey, Virgie, Angie, Lloyd, Dodi, Tony Bennett (he didn't heart the part about himself), etc., etc., etc. Even the children, Tony and Dee Dee, got bits and pieces.

Thanks to my family, whom I love dearly.

Thanks to dear Wendell Shackelford, who patiently helped me put the book together.

Thanks to you in show business from whom I learned so much.

Thanks to those I've caused pain, and those who caused me pain (we both learned).

Thanks to Doc, who knows how I really emerged from darkness to light.

And I hope I did what President Arthur E. Turner, of Northwood Institute, Midland, Michigan, told me: Write a book that will be worthwhile, so you can help others.

This I have tried to do.

Pearl Bailey

LIST OF ILLUSTRATIONS

Papa

Mama

Pearl Bailey at the age of three

"The One and Only" Bill Bailey

Eura with Tony Bellson

Virgie

Dee Dee Bellson at four months

Josephine Premice, Diahann Carroll, Pearl Bailey, and Juanita Hall in *House of Flowers*

Pearl Bailey and Sammy Davis, Jr., in a scene from *Porgy and Bess*

Pearl Bailey and Nat King Cole on set of *St. Louis Blues*

Pearl Bailey in kitchen on ranch at Apple Valley, California, taken during filming of *Porgy and Bess* in 1958

Pearl, Louie, and Tony Bellson at Las Vegas airport

Eura, Mrs. Bellson, Pearl, Louie, and Tony in Las Vegas

Pearl Bailey onstage at the Flamingo in Las Vegas

Pearl Bailey, Joe Louis, and the Valenzuela boys in Las Vegas

Pearl Bailey and Don Redman at a recording session

Pearl Bailey at her fiftieth birthday party, with "Peetney" Redman

All the things that seemed ugly have been washed away by the beauty I've found in living with humanity, and so some things that I might have written cannot now be told because the picture of these moments has dimmed.

I do not want my book just to tell about things that happened to Pearl. I really want this book to tell some of the things I've learned about life. It's not so easy to write down. This is new to me. I don't always have the kind of words I want to express myself. My hands have always been my words in a way. Sometimes waving your hand a certain way is better than words. This time it's all words—no waving of the hands.

So I mean to concentrate on what I have gained from life, and not just on events. How sad, just when so many have put on bifocals to absorb all the "goody goody gumdrops" of this life. The "events" of my life are important only when they have brought me along to my present outlook on life.

In reading a lot of books lately, the lives of this or that one, I notice they say things happened "because of" race, religion, or creed. Perhaps this is so, but wearing no label, being of the people, for the people, all under the judgment of God, I can only feel that what has happened to me has been, and will be, because it's my destiny—as your life is yours.

The Raw
Pearl

1

I don't remember much about Newport News. Mama says I walked and talked at eight months; I know that at nineteen or twenty months I was imitating my elders, sitting on the porch saying "Howdo" to the passing crowd.

Mama had not intended to have another child. She tells of a strange lady coming to the door, predicting the arrival of an unusual baby girl; Mama says she laughed. But three and a half years later Pearlie Mae arrived. Papa had planned on a boy to be named Dick, so I inherited that as a nickname. It's the only thing my father ever called me.

There are four of us: Virgie, Willie, Eura, and Dick (me). When I was three, Mama let me go to school with Eura and Willie. They must have been in the first or second grade. Mama has told me that I'd run my finger along the pages of their school books and "read" perfectly. Of course, I would be on the wrong page; I had memorized the story.

One day when Mama thought I was at school, the door opened and in came my godmother, Mrs. Minnie, bringing me. Where had I been? Hiding behind a tree because a button was off my coat. Funny, now I detest dressing up except when I really have to.

About this time, there was a fad called the Buster Brown haircut. Mama thought it would look good on me. Off to the barber shop I went, but I told the man to cut *all* my hair off. He assumed, I guess, that since I was only three, if I had made it to the corner someone must have sent me. He cut it off. Now, my ears had been pierced at two, so when Mama discovered me I was in bed, bald as an eagle with earrings. Mama went to the shop real angry, but after the man explained, what could she say? We all went to Suffolk, Virginia, to visit my grandmother and everyone wanted to see the little boy with the bald head, dress, and earrings.

We stayed in Virginia in the same house until I was four, with Dr. Scott on one side of us and C. C. Cunningham, the undertaker, on the other.

From Virginia the Bailey clan moved to Washington, D.C. I can remember rolling Easter eggs at the zoo and playing in Lincoln Memorial Pool. What I was doing in there, heaven only knows. I couldn't swim—God just kept me floating around for the future, I guess. We were a happy family then; how and when the misery set in I can't say.

I've always looked at Mama as a great personality. She has the ability to charm a snake. Even when she is in pain she smiles. Papa was the opposite. When things were wrong, oh, would you know it! At times I've admired his frankness; he called a spade a spade. Other times I've thought Mama's method was better. In later years I found her way best for making and keeping friends. Papa talked in parables with a great deal of wisdom; he also had a sense of humor. He used to say, "Season your words." Too bad he didn't practice it as often as he said it. My question to him was, "Season with what?" Mama used sugar. Sometimes her words were too sweet; a lot of people don't like that much sugar. Papa used a lot of salt; he poured it in the wound—and there we children sat, in between the two.

They were both handsome, and we've been blessed as their children to get a share of each. Time has passed, my knowledge has grown; so thanks to them for the sugar and salt, to which I've added a few spices of my own.

Papa always had some kind of old car. He never seemed to get a new one. And I remember we went around the reservoir in Papa's open-topped car on Sundays as a treat. The Lincoln and Republic theatres are located on U Street, and that's where our friends would be after Sunday school. Everybody would be catching the Sunday matinee, and we came from church (remember, Papa was a reverend), made this whirlwind tour, then, if we were extra good, we could go to the theatre. I remember once all four tires of the car were gone, and here we came down U Street, with Papa telling us all to sit up straight, and, boy, we wanted to get underneath something, because all our friends going into the movie were watching and we were just making it, on the dern four rims. Mama always had too much pride to make that trip—and I don't blame her.

While the Lincoln and Republic theatres were on U Street, where all the fancy people strolled, the Dunbar, Broadway, and a few others were on Seventh Street. We were not allowed to go to the Midcity and the Elmo; they were a bit rough. Ten cents was the price of admission everywhere, and you usually got a few extra pennies to spend. (You'd add to your pot by not putting all you had in the Sunday-school basket.) Mary Pickford, Douglas Fairbanks, Tom Mix, Hoot Gibson, Clara Bow, Lon Chaney, Chaplin (the King), Valentino—stars too numerous to mention. Heavens, I left out my doll, Ramon Novarro! My sister Virgie's favorite was John Gilbert. In those days, we had the serials. Each week someone was left in a burning canyon, in the clutches of an octopus, or in a lion's mouth in the jungle. The following week the situation was cleared up, only to worsen again in the last fifteen minutes. Every child left the theatre minus a few fingernails and in mortal fear that his hero, or heroine, was dead (until next week).

Willie and Eura would spend a portion of their money on the way to the show. I kept mine so I'd have enough to get something to munch on. There was often a shortage of ticket money when we got to the box office, so they would ask for part of mine. I'd say, "No," and start inside; they'd say, "The Lord loves a cheerful giver," or "A bird may fly high, but he's got to come down to eat." That always got under my skin, so I'd lend them the change. It's still pretty much the same now with people. If a person likes something I've got, he is welcome to it. But some kinds of giving can be a mistake—now I try to give folks not what they can *use* but what they *need*.

People of the theatre give freely. To do this in the wrong way will make your loved ones draw away. Keep it simple and real. The famous say, "Take my hand, let me help," even though some of them might want to say, "May I take yours?"

At times there have been folks, even in my family, who felt they "could use" some of the money I was making. For a while I tried to buy their love that way. But I found out that was foolish.

Sunday also seemed to be Argument Day. Papa and Mama regularly had a red-hot one going right after church. Then Mama's flat steamer trunk used to get pushed out in the hall. Mama would push it back in. Peace for six days, then Sunday again. What the basic trouble was I've never known. One Sunday the trunk went out; Mama and children followed.

We moved to 1207 Fifth Street. Papa would come by from our old home at 1300 Florida Avenue, bring the groceries, see us, and again an argument would start. I'm sure then it was about a reconciliation, but Mama was through. In later years she didn't have any animosity toward Papa, and kept the deepest respect for him; it was just one of those things.

At that time there was a cousin living with us who was my father's sister's child, named James. His father and mother were dead, and my brother Willie and he used to really "have it." It seemed like they always picked Sunday mornings, too. Every single Sunday morning my brother and James would get into *something*. I'll never forget one Sunday they went up to a grocery store on the corner and, being young boys, they snitched some Baby Ruths out of the store. Willie sent James in to get them while he waited outside. Somebody from across the street caught them, and naturally James got the blame for it. Actually, he went in and got the candy not because he really wanted it but because he loved my brother so much.

My mother would invariably give Willie the whipping—because, I imagine, she didn't want James to think she was protecting her son. One day when Bill, as usual, got the whipping, I think it must have gone a little too deep. We had a wood stove in the kitchen, and a cot. James slept in the kitchen on the cot. Well, that night when James had on his long underwear (and you know how they're made), my brother just waited until James got ready to say his prayers and stuck the straightening comb that you fix your hair with through the grate of the stove. Once the iron was hot, all we heard was, "Our Father who art in heaven, oh my God, Aunt Mary!" because my brother had taken the hot comb and stuck it inside James's flap. Oh boy, Mama really warmed Willie later.

Easter Sunday that year was a very important day. It's a day that I don't want to remember as a thing of ugliness, but I'll never forget it. On Easter Sunday morning, my father came over. Mama and Papa had been separated for some time by then, and a person has a right when he or she is separated to have a friend. Well, Mr. Walter, the man who is now my stepfather, was there visiting. A lady named Betty used to stay with us. We called her Miss Betty, and she was a friend of my mother's. Miss Betty and my father came in the door—Papa had come right from church, the early-morning service, and he had the Bible in his hand. He came in, came around through the kitchen to the parlor, laid the Bible on the mantelpiece, and started in with the gentleman. There was quite a scene! And that's when my mother decided to move completely out of town. I guess Mama thought, you know, this could only lead to violence or something, and she left and went to Philadelphia. And so every Easter Sunday I wake up the first thing, even this Easter, and I remember that scene.

The court gave Mama the privilege of taking Virgie, because she was eighteen and could help Mama; but, bless her, Virgie decided it was best for her to remain and keep an eye on us. At no time was Mama running away from us; the move was just better for all concerned. And then Papa loved us, too. Today I can realize it must have been a big decision for them both. We thrived with Papa, but of course we missed Mama.

Papa was preaching at the "House of Prayer," and we went every night. Bishop Grace was head of all these churches. (Papa was one of the oldest Elders when he died in 1966, at eighty-four.)

At this particular House of Prayer, some of the members lived upstairs. When it was announced that Daddy Grace was coming to visit, everybody went wild. Carpets were rolled out, the band tuned up—trumpets, trombones and all. The soldiers (I called them that, but actually they were members in uniform) lined up on each side with swords held up (I doubt if they were sharp). Childlike, I thought, "What do they need the weapons for?" And as a grownup I still ask the question.

Though everyone put on their finery every Sunday, when Daddy Grace came they got ragged out for sure. Somehow I could never call him "Daddy," just "Bishop." He had shoulder-length hair, a goatee, and was so elegant! The collection basket was filled; hankies and combs, blessed by Daddy Grace, were sold.

The House of Prayer is a holy and sanctified church; they really shout. As in the Bible, they declare themselves speaking in tongues; they also get so happy sometimes that they fall "under the Power." When the older folks shouted, sometimes their money would fall out of their pockets; that was the children's cue. We got extremely happy, started to shout, fell under the Power but on top of the money. While I was on the floor, I used to hear them say, "Look at Elder Bailey's girl! So happy, isn't that wonderful!" Brother! I had to stay down there for Financial Gain. I hope I'm forgiven that sin.

Remember, everyone who lived upstairs could hear that music and, believe me, it was swinging! The children were dancing their dance upstairs, and the old ones were shouting down below. Where did rock and roll come from? It came from the music of the Negro churches, definitely.

Just listen to the beat and go to one of the churches and see if you don't hear the same thing.

Life went on for us in D.C., but Bill got restless and one day he took off. He had an old bicycle, and he left for Philadelphia. (Now, Virgie wrote most of the letters to Mama, so she had the address and Bill didn't know it.) The next day we received a wire from Mama; he was there. Without any sure information, he'd pedaled up there and landed on a street he thought was right. Having no address, he went to a drugstore on the corner and asked the druggist did he know a lady with very deep dimples (which Mama has), named Ella Mae, and who might live in that block. The druggist said he had a lady that fitted that description working for him. He called her Mary. Fortunately, she lived down the street. It was raining like mad, so the man gave him an umbrella and the approximate number of the house. Willie went there and rang the bell. A lady on the third floor looked out the window and asked who it was. When Willie heard the voice he started to cry; of all things, it was Mama. How strange! It was late, and no one else in the whole house woke up.

Bill stayed with Mama for a few months, had a little job; then that restlessness again. He decided that because I was the baby I belonged with Mama. He returned to D.C. In the meantime, Virgie had gotten married and moved, so Eura was head of the house. She must have been fourteen, almost fifteen. Willie, Virgie, and Eura discussed taking me to Mama. One Saturday night Papa went to church in his marvelous "Tin Lizzie" Ford, and Willie said, "Tomorrow you go to Mama."

Sunday morning early we crept down the stairs, out the back alley, and over to Virgie's, where my suitcase was. Every squeak on the stairs sounded like thunder, and we had to pass Papa sleeping on the second floor. We caught the train and arrived in Philly around noon. Mama didn't know Willie's plan, so what a surprise when she opened the door and, bless him, Willie said, "Mama, I've got Dick."

That same evening he returned to Washington to be with Eura. My father said, "I would have let her go, had you asked." They say he cried. Soon after, Bill came back to

Philadelphia with Eura. We owe you our thanks, Willie.

Mama was married again, to Mr. Walter, a nice man (they're still together), and we became a happy family. I went to the Joseph Singerly School, right across from us on Twenty-second Street.

I remember a wonderful teacher, a lady named Mrs. Faison. This was a fine lady, and she liked me very much. (Of course, teachers sometimes used to hit you with the ruler and all, and I had my share of that, too.) One day Mrs. Faison came in and gave me a box; it was my birthday. When I got home and opened it, I've never been so thrilled in my life—it was a pair of white pure-silk stockings. I'd never had a pair of silk stockings. Why she gave them to me I don't know; I guess she just liked me.

I put on these stockings and walked to the Catholic Church. I had seen the church from outside, but had never been in it. As a child, it wasn't so much a faith that I had. I wanted to go to that pretty church because I'd heard Catholics talking about the Mass and all, and it sounded fascinating. In my heart it seemed a sanctified and holy church, in a different way from Papa's. So, with my beautiful white stockings, in I went. I followed what I saw the other people do—when they kneel, you know, there before the candles—so I kneeled. Well, when I got up there was a big hole in the knee of my white silk stockings, and that ended my Catholic religion!

I used to go and play Blind Man's Buff with my friend Marcella, and my deadline to be in was 10 P.M. I was about thirteen years old, but that was it. And when I didn't make that deadline, I really got it. One night I'd gone up to Marcella's to play, and when I came in it must have been ten-fifteen or ten-thirty. My mother was a woman who would say, "I'm going to get you," and she promised a long time, but when she did get you, she *got* you. And this particular night I came in and she was writing a letter. We had one of those sofas that open out into a bed, and she said to me something she'd never said in her life. She said, "You just take off everything, because tonight I'm going to just kill you." She had never told us to take *all* our clothes off for a whipping. This was going to be something sensational.

I got in that sofa bed, and her back was to me and she was writing, and all I could do was lay there and wonder, "If I close my eyes, when is this terrible thing going to happen." The whipping didn't make me as nervous as the fact that I was naked, so I thought she was really going to kill me. Finally I couldn't stand it any longer, and I just jumped straight up in the bed, a little naked kid, and said, "Kill me, Mama, just kill me now. Kill me while I'm wide awake." And I could see her shoulders shaking. She was laughing at me.

We moved then to Van Pelt Street, and the ten o'clock deadline was still in force. I had a close friend named Elizabeth Harris near the corner. The Harrises were a very *elegant* family. Somebody in her family was a teacher, and this was what you call elegant, you know, a teacher in the family or a doctor. I was about fourteen and Elizabeth was about sixteen, so she could do a little courting, but I wasn't allowed to. Of course, I always went to the store the long way around; I'd stop by my girl friend's house, pick her up, and go by the corner (where the little boys would stand, you see) before I could get back. To get a pound of sugar usually took me about an hour.

Up and down Diamond Street there was a big graveyard. It started at Twenty-second Street and went all the way across to Twenty-fifth, and at Twenty-fifth and Diamond was a ball park (where, incidentally, I happened to see this wonderful catcher, and they say he was the greatest catcher of all time—Josh Gibson). The Homestead Grays used to come there and play, and the Birmingham Clowns. Now, along the graveyard was a wall, and as children we used to sit on that wall to play "Counting Cars." By this time you could tell the make of a car, you know; you knew a Ford from a Chevrolet, and that's about what they had. We would sit there at night and call out, "That's *my* car."

One night Elizabeth and I were out there counting the cars. Two little boys had wandered by, too, and we were all just innocently playing, just sitting up on the wall there. We had such a good time, but finally the cars got fewer and fewer. There weren't that many cars in those days, anyhow. So I jumped down and said, "Gee, Elizabeth, there's so few cars and I'm getting cold. Let's go home." A man was coming along the street and I asked him, "Mister, what time is it?" He looked at his watch and said, "It's a quarter to two." Well, I tell you, if I ever died I died then. I had never *heard* of a quarter to two. I'd never been awake at two in the morning. Even now, at this age, I can't forget how scared I was. I was paralyzed, really. I said, "Mister, you don't mean quarter to *two*," and he said, "Quarter to two," and I was just frozen. I didn't know whether to go home or run away or *what* to do. Elizabeth and I started home.

I wanted to be brave, but I knew that it was death for me—I was already figuring the size of the box and everything. I was going along and now these two little boys, whoever they were, were skipping along behind. I was hitting back at them, "Go away!" because, above all, I had to turn that last corner and I did not want those little boys behind me.

My mother would always say, "Don't you have a baby!" Oh boy, I could see it, and they were still skipping. There was a big nursery on the corner and we lived three doors above that. My mother was famous for not coming to the door, and we never had a key—we had to ring the bell, that alerted Mama to look at the clock. I knew she would look out the window, because that's Philadelphia style—you hear the bell and you look out the window.

Just as I was about halfway to the nursery, I saw that little head out the window of our house. I said, "Go back, little boys!" It was obvious to me she had seen me. She must have been relieved that I was alive and not dead or something, but she was *angry*. I could hear her all the way down the street. She had a habit of saying, "Come on, madam, come right on, because I am going to *kill* you." That was her famous expression, "I am going to kill you." What she meant was, "I am going to *give* it to you." She said, "You little boys might as well skip back, because I am going to kill her." She's saying this out of her window, and it's penetrating the quiet street. The street was dark; nobody, not even the grownups, was up at two at night. So we came on, and tried to be brave.

My mother was very fond of Elizabeth and her family, so Elizabeth stopped and said, "We were just . . ." Mama said, "Go home, Elizabeth, because I'm sure your mother is going to kill you, too, so go home!" She didn't want to hear anything from Elizabeth, either. Elizabeth was trying to save me a little bit, but when she heard this she left. I was standing on the top step, and I said, "Mama"—as if to help her—"throw me the key." You know, she kept looking down on me. She wouldn't come down; that's the part that was frightening. She just kept looking at me, saying, "You don't *need* a key, young lady, you won't need a key, because *I*"—and she's pointing at me—"am going to *kill* you."

I waited awhile, and I heard the window go down. She was coming down those stairs. She opened the door, and I had to go by her, so I did a real ballet step. I just skipped in, and when I did (honest to goodness, it's a wonder I've got any sense), she klunked me on the back of my head. I tell you, oh boy, she really gave it to me. Now it was what was I doing with the little boys, and I would have a baby and so forth! I never got out the fact that I was counting cars, because she didn't give me time. At that point in my life I started to make that deadline; ten o'clock began to mean something to me.

Mama bought a house on Twenty-third Street, where she still lives and where my career started. While living there, I used to go out to "Jew Town," around Thirtieth and Diamond. All Hebrew people lived there, though I can't see why it needed a title. (People are still labeling, and it's so distasteful.) On Fridays I would go to scrub and clean to make spending change. Mama didn't send us; it was my ambition to work, so she said okay. (Today I clean my own house, with the help of my husband and children. I'm thankful Lou and I both have mothers who are fantastic housekeepers.) I was planning to be a schoolteacher, and this would help me to earn my way.

Around then, brother Willie was getting a big reputation in show business as a tap dancer, and we were proud of him. The Baileys had a star in the family. Willie would come home in his fancy car, and it was like Christmas every time he arrived. He'd bring different performers to the house for dinner; even the neighbors began to look forward to his playing the Pearl Theatre, so they could see the celebrities: the world-famous Berry Brothers, Jigsaw Jackson, Mr. Sydney Easton, Miss Ada Ward, and many famous musicians. It was a gay household when Bill brought people home. None of this had any influence on my finally going into the business, because we all had sung and danced from the beginning, with no lessons. (Even Mama.)

On Sundays the Lincoln Theatre at Broad and South Street had a "Kiddie Hour," on radio. Stump and Stumpy, Dottie Saulters, Moke and Poke—many good performers got their start there. A lot were picked by the bandleaders to sing with them. One lady was Ida James, who sang with Earl Hines.

Willie used to urge me to go down and show off what he said was my exceptional talent. I thought I wasn't interested in the theatre, and anyway I was too shy. I'd sing and dance like a demon around the house, but to do it in front of people? Never.

But one night Mama sent me to the Pearl Theatre to tell Willie to come home to dinner. At fifteen, you want to see it all, and I had never been backstage. I gave the message to him (he was rehearsing a number to do the following week with the chorus girls), then lingered. Though he wanted me to be in the theatre, he still didn't want his baby sister hanging around backstage. He ordered me to leave. When I refused, he gave me a lick.

How I burned, especially since I considered myself quite the lady. Then I had a brilliant idea. Why not return later in the evening? It was going to be Amateur Night, a wonderful chance to embarrass him in front of people and get even. When you're young, the silliest notions seem the greatest achievements. Bill meant a lot to me, and I'd never dreamed he would run me out of the theatre. So now he really ran into a tiger. I went back and arrived as the last contestant was going on. Since they knew me, they let me go on after her. My songs were "The Talk of the

Town" and the masterpiece "Poor Butterfly." It's still my favorite song. Being a dancer also, I threw in a fast buck dance and received a big hand. The other contestants were brought out, the master of ceremonies placed his hand over each head in turn, and I won. I won the dern contest—and standing in the wings, beaming, was Willie.

They gave me a five-dollar prize and the offer of a week's work. High school let out at two o'clock, so I could make the matinee, do my homework in between shows, and get plenty of rest at night. The big hurdle was Mama. Willie talked to her, and he was good at twisting her around his finger. The next hurdle was getting dear sister Eura (who by now was a singing waitress and owned a couple of precious evening gowns from the thrift shop) to lend me a dress. This task was not easy, until Mama put her foot down. One I asked, and one I got.

Instead of talking with Willie, the man at the theatre (smart cookie) cornered me and offered thirty dollars a week. Big-shot I took it. The chorus girls were only making twenty-two dollars and fifty cents so I was in a class all alone. At fifteen and a half that was a lot of money. I had it all figured out: two-thirds would go to Mama and one-third to me. (Little did I know that the theatre was on its last legs.)

The shows started on Friday and on Monday all the acts would draw some of their money. Because we didn't have unions then, this was a safety measure. (Also, most of the actors always needed a bit of change.) I knew this, but when Monday came around, the man approached me again with an offer to remain another week. Gee whiz! A smash I was, held over; why not wait and get the money in a lump? Sixty bucks! What had I done to deserve such a blessing? I accepted.

The following Wednesday, when I made that dramatic entrance into the alley leading to the stage door, I saw all the acts standing there. They were all staring at the beautiful padlock on the gate leading down to the door. It was a sight I shall not forget. Whether the loss of the money or the fact that those portals were closed on a dream hurt me more, I can't recall now. My mother gave me a lecture on collecting salary, and I have followed her advice ever since. She said, "Never start the second week until you've been paid for the first one." She said the law would ask me if the man didn't pay me for the first week why did I do the second. How much law she knows I can't say, but it makes awful good sense, so I've stuck with it.

School suddenly lost its charm for me now. I was often late, homework was skipped, and my behavior became poor. There was a purpose: get thrown out so maybe I would get a chance to go back to that land of enchantment, the theatre. Mama had to go to Virginia on business; she did not believe in leaving us alone, but my stepfather was there and he was strict, too. One thing she didn't count on, though—how extra fond of me my stepfather was. So I successfully got myself suspended in her absence and went past the allotted time before giving him the note to appear at school to save me from being thrown out for good. Ella Mae (Mama) almost did me in, I assure you, and the school would have taken me back, but Fate was kind to me, the vixen. Summer holidays came.

Every summer since we'd moved to Philadelphia I'd gone to Washington to attend to Virgie's babies. By now her tribe had reached a total of three. For this chore I was paid one dollar and a half per week while Virgie did outside work. I fixed dinner, cleaned diapers, whatever I was told. Then, still wanting to be a schoolteacher, I would take all the children into the basement and teach them school work. Oh, ambition was mine, even when I was very young.

Even though we lived apart from time to time, we children managed to stay pretty close. Which is surprising, because we really were all different. So far, I haven't said too much about Eura.

Eura was "the weeper." We used to call her the weeper because she was the crybaby of the group. Virgie, the staid one, was called stingy. We always thought Virgie was very close. She probably was not really stingy, but she just wanted to make sure she had a little something hidden, let's put it that way. You can't really blame her for that. She had the responsibility of her children.

But Eura was the weeper and the soft one. It seemed like she could sit in a corner, and if two people were over in another corner talking, Eura had the idea that they were discussing her. In other words, she's a highly sensitive person.

Later in my life I've realized that she was really going around trying to help people in her way. And yet, it seemed like wherever Eura was, that's where the seat of trouble was. She was always fighting trouble. It seemed that wherever she went, she was going to be hurt because she had so much tenderness in her—she's a darling sister. Eura was trying to solve things, but the strength she gave was never appreciated. A poem often comes back to me—one that Eura learned in school and recited at home. The part I remember best was, "What is your head? Is it a hat rack or a thinking machine?" I've tried to make mine a thinking machine, and though I adore hats they've never squeezed the brain so tight I couldn't think for myself. I often wanted to remind Eura of that—let people stand on their own.

Eura, I guess at one time, was about the best-looking girl in all Philadelphia, or one of the best. She had gorgeous legs and a figure and everything. My mother always said, "However hard I have to work, I will put things in the home for you to enjoy. I don't want my daughters standing on corners. When you get ready to have a boy friend, I want you to bring him into the house," and this sort of thing. But being a glamour girl of that day, Eura would take these little walks, especially on Berks Street, which was where the barbershop my stepfather went to to get his hair cut and everything was. Naturally, like in every barbershop, the young fellows sort of stood around there. Well, up and down Eura made these little walks; you know, she'd get up a little early and get very prissy.

I'll never forget the 30th of May one year. Eura was about fifteen or sixteen, and my mother had warned her about passing up and down in front of the barbershop— because men talk about you, she said, when they see you go by a barbershop too much. But Eura had disappeared that morning as usual. My mother got up and headed for

Eura's territory. Someone had told Mama they saw Eura going down Berks Street, and Mama knew exactly what she was doing, parading. Mama disappeared out of the house, and the next thing I heard were these feet on the stairs, the running, the horrible running, and behind Eura was my mother with the ironing cord. My mother had run her all the way home from the barbershop and straight up the stairs. Eura ran in the bedroom, locked the door, and got under the bed.

I imagine Eura won't ever forget that day, but my mother just wanted us to have a good life. It was a certain self-discipline that just had to be there or you weren't a lady. Because she always taught us that a man could do anything and still wake up the next morning and be a man, but a woman couldn't.

After my show-biz debut I sort of lost interest in going to Washington to baby-sit for Virgie. The salary was less, too, than the thirty a week I could make on the stage, and the glamour of show business was not to be replaced by feeding children oatmeal. But I was still only a child, and there was nothing for me to do but accept my fate. Yet I had tasted something, and it was delicious.

Willie had appeared at various well-known places in New York, and on his trips home he had stories to tell about this city of mystery. He'd have our eyes bulging, trying to imagine those tall buildings that disappeared into the sky. When I returned from the summer with Virgie, Willie took me to New York for a short visit with him and his lovely wife, Jessie Scott, who was also in the theatre and a fantastic dancer. She and Bill worked at the Ubangi Club, and I saw Gladys Bentley, Moms Mabley (funniest woman alive, no script but her own), and many major stars. Under the Cotton Club there was a theatre, the Dunbar. Once in the daytime I walked up the stairs of that famous club, then came down and sat on the curb so I could take in the height of the buildings. The Lafayette Theatre was at an end, but the Alhambra, the Harlem Opera House, and the Apollo were the big buns. On that trip I got a big thrill when Bill bought me my first "expensive" shoes; they came from Wise's, three ninety-five, really high class.

Sometimes we went to Mom Baker's, Lulu Belle's, or Jenny Lou's to eat; all the show folks dropped by these spots at one time or the other. I can't explain the feeling I had when I looked at the real greats. I didn't eat much, I just stared and hoped they would look up and give me the warmth of their smiles, or that maybe I'd overhear them talking about some great happening in the theatre.

As usual, Willie recommended an amateur hour to me, to show my talents. It was not a cinch to go on these shows. Everyone on them was nearly professional already. I was dressed to go to the Harlem Opera House, got there too late, so went down the street to the Apollo. They had Erskine Hawkins' orchestra as the headliner of the show. They were called the Bama State Collegians, and "Tuxedo Junction" was their big song. But when the hand was held over the heads, I won again for "In My Solitude," arrangement homemade. Maybe my nice appearance helped, too. I'm grateful I didn't go down the street to the Opera House. I doubt if I would have made it there, for that night a young girl walked on that stage, opened her mouth, and the audience that had started to snicker ended up cheering. The girl sang "Judy." Her name was Ella Fitzgerald. She won, and that voice will go down in history. The sound till now has not been matched.

In the middle of the winter that year, I went back to Virgie's to care for the children. A new baby was on the way, and my interest was high because the baby was going to be born at home. January 20th, the screams started and I sat in the living room listening to the wails. Then I was called up. I picked this tiny creature up and started rubbing oil on her and humming a song as I held her. The first granddaughter for Mama. I called her "Sister."

Soon after, I went to catch the show at the Howard Theatre and, as always, went down the side alley to watch the show people come out. The girls wore a lot of mascara beading, and their lashes looked ten feet long to me, just gorgeous. All of them spoke; they recognized me as Bill's little sister. One mentioned that Noble Sissle, of "Shuffle Along" fame, was thinking of using a boy-and-girl dance act, to go into New York. Not a great one, just a fill-in between chorus numbers. Bill knew a boy called Blackie Johnson, who danced around Washington, so I asked him to join up with me, and we'd try out for Sissle. We got the job. I could dance, but I'm sure being Bill's sister didn't hurt.

We ended up in Indian costumes, doing a fast dance across the stage. Papa would have liked that. (He was half Creek, so he would have thought I'd gone back to the tribe.) We played three weeks, but when we got to New York, the producer, Addison Carey, announced our act was out. Blackie, who danced so well, seemed to freeze onstage before him. Mr. Carey said he could use a girl in the chorus, and I could have that job. I took it. I was in show business, making twenty-two bucks a week, and passing the dressing rooms of the greats. Not being a baller, I simply danced my fanny off and ate like a horse. Some weeks I ate the whole salary, except for rent money. Clothes never meant that much to me.

Philly loomed in sight (big time) and I got jobs around home. Pearlie Mae was swinging, but making it home every night. Mama would still have no foolishness about staying out. I wasn't old enough yet. Soon the calls came to go north—not to Maine, but to Pottsville, Pennsylvania. Such a packing job you've never seen, finally leaving home for foreign shores. Anyone would have thought I was headed for Broadway. Well, it felt like it to me. Mama gave instructions I'd heard a million times. Remember, I wasn't going where Virgie could keep an eye on me, or New York where Willie could watch; I would be alone in a place Mama hadn't read about, nor did she have a law to fit its morals. If she had guessed what a wild spot I was headed into, I'd never have left Philly.

The only thing I knew about the coal regions was that people got bootleg coal from there. At least they said they did. When you got a ton of coal in town it cost fifteen dollars, and when they brought it from the mountains (Scranton, Wilkes-Barre, Hazleton, and all those mining towns), it cost thirteen bucks. You shoveled it into the cellar yourself or gave the guy an extra two bucks for the labor. It was too dramatic to have anyone go to the bus with me, so I headed for the hills alone, with a half-filled suitcase and hope in my heart that the people would like me. My, my, my, the places I passed through on my long journey (all in all, it must have taken three hours). When the man said "Pottsville" my heart stopped. Little did I dream I'd get an education here that school would never teach.

The address was the Manhattan Café on Minersville Street; salary, fifteen dollars and tips. The room was free. It was on the same floor as the club, and later I was happy to be there. The rest of the rooms in the town were for rent, but by everyone, for everyone and anyone, and the purpose: *mamma mia!*

2

Pottsville, Pennsylvania, at that time was wide open. All of the coal region was known for sporting houses, or what was commonly called the red-light district. (They really did have red lights in the windows.) Minersville Street was the busiest street in Pottsville; the girls even jumped on the running boards of the cars to catch "tricks."

The pimps had their stables (a sizable number of "ladies of the evening"). Some had quite an array. The bigger the stable, the finer the gentleman. Hah! The mayor of the town was into everything, a real swinger. Someone would send out word they were going to raid the houses, and a lot of girls would leave Pottsville and go to Scranton or Wilkes-Barre, about fifty miles away. The fine was approximately twenty-six dollars and they didn't want to pay it. A day or two after the raid they would return, only to be visited by The Man, who would demand his fee. The girls would tell him they had been out of town, but it mattered not, they had to pay.

To my young, inexperienced eyes, there was a touch of humor about these pimps and their girls. It was something to see a girl come into the cabaret with a black eye, when the boy friend had beat her the night before for not bringing in enough dough. She'd tip you a big fat dollar (which was a lot, considering that a performer's salary was from twelve to eighteen dollars a week) to sing "My Man" or "When a Woman Loves a Man." The pimps really tipped the entertainers lavishly, whether you would go for the "business" or not. When they found out you were a nice girl only out to do show business, they respected you. Nobody was vicious, though every now and then there was a battle between the girls over their man. These people were just in business.

If you wanted to go into these houses and see the trade at work, you were welcome. My taste was not for that sort of thing. Mama's teaching held up well always, thank God. Some girls resented the entertainers because their fellows gave them the eye, so you had to tread softly. There were some pretty rough ones, and jail meant nothing to them. They could get out in five minutes.

Don't think that everyone in the town was in "the business." It was a town of nice families, too, and all nationalities—Syrian, Polish, Lithuanian, Irish, Negro—and folks got along. They just knew their town and accepted it, each one going his own way.

To make an extra buck I would straighten the girls' hair. For this I was paid seventy-five cents, and I did a thriving business. The Syrians taught me to play knock rummy, in the back of a tiny local restaurant that was closed for regular business but open for pool and card games, so I learned to shoot pool, too. Then I had a brilliant idea. Why not open the restaurant and have a business on the side? Mama had taught me to cook, so I could serve my customers well. But the big mistake about the whole thing was that my customers were the ones that taught me how to get rid of my money. Pretty soon my profits were "eaten up"—in knock rummy. Soon the "Café Owner" was only singing for her supper again. I found out that show biz was my trade, not hash slinging; but it's good to know you can sling hash and not be too proud to.

The Manhattan was the meeting place of the Sports and

the Seekers of Pleasure. We put on our show and they put on theirs. Actually, you couldn't call it a show. There were four or five singers and dancers, a comedian, and an M.C. Each performer would take his turn, and in between the girl singers did "ups." "Ups" meant going from table to table singing the same song. Sometimes the customers put money on the table and you took it off. No! my sweet, not with your hands but with your thighs. You pulled up your dress to a certain height and grabbed the money off the corner of the table. I must admit some sisters pulled them up rather high, and the guys loved it. This was done not only in the coal region; it happened all over. Some of you may even recall the small dimes and how hard they were to snatch off.

There were no microphones. As Paul Laurence Dunbar said in his famous poem "When Malindy Sings," you just opened your mouth and hollered. The show started with an opening number in which everyone participated; then everyone did a solo specialty.

We seldom had musical arrangements. When we did, it wasn't over three pieces for rhythm: piano, bass, and drums. You had your repertoire on a piece of paper and strangely enough, everyone had the same songs. "Nagasaki" was the famous number. Another was "I Could Do Most Anything for You," and, naturally, any other song that talked about women sacrificing for men. Some girls drank and mixed with the customers, and they cleaned up on tips. Some also did a bit of side business for pocket change. They had these jobs sewed up, and they could make it tough for a new entertainer. In fact, they made it tougher to stay in town than the sporting girls did.

Once in Scranton, Pennsylvania, one of the greatest pimps got carried away with me. I was too scared and dumb for him to do anything, but he enjoyed treating me like a charming toy. He never approached me; he'd just tip me big when I sang at his table, and inside he must have been smiling at this child who was blushing every time she looked at him. He was handsome, but I assure you I had no intentions of going to work. E-flat and A-flat were about as much as I understood—and of course I dug looking at a good-looking guy. I didn't drink, so he'd buy me cokes and pickled eggs and pretzels. I'd eat some of my goodies and save the rest to take to my three-dollar room for my next day's breakfast. My, my! How could I forget the purple pickled eggs and pretzels for which Pennsylvania is so famous?

In Wilkes-Barre I lived at Evelyn's under the bridge and worked at Jake's Town Tavern at Ninety-ninth and State Street. Living on our salary and tips was really something, but prices were different then. I spent fifteen dollars a week this way: three for rent, three for board, nine dollars left for clothes, and don't forget Mama got at least a dollar and a half. She didn't ask; she just deserved it because she was Mama.

The only time Mama ever got a glimpse of any of this was once, back in Pottsville, when I asked her to come. One day after rehearsal my friend Ida and I had decided to go to a movie. She had on a weird hat, and I turned around to laugh at it and fell down a steep flight of stairs. I sprained my ankle and was lucky not to be killed. (By then I had progressed to having a room in one of the local houses, my own room. Most of the houses had rooms—transient—and you could never make a bet the landlady wasn't a madam. No one bothered you, though, and you bothered no one.) Well, my foot got worse and I was getting scared, so Mama and Mr. Walter drove up from Philadelphia. This was the first and only time in my entire career that I sent for Mama. She, being an immaculate housekeeper, looked more at the lady's house than at my foot. My room was clean, but the rest of the house was not up to par. The bath was just off the kitchen, and that didn't sit well with her, either. Mama's voice rang loud and clear, and I knew the landlady heard her. "Pearlie, if I ever catch you in a dirty place like this again [then came the great line], *I'll kill you*. Remember something always: I want you to live in the best place you can afford, eat well, and if there is anything left, send some to Mama." So far, Mama, I've listened.

A lot of people might think this must have been a pretty frightening experience or an unhappy life for a girl my age, away from home for the first time. But I didn't feel that way. I was someone who went out there with something—not so much a sureness of my talent, but a sureness that this was where I wanted to go and where I belonged. God had given me enough to pay the price.

Soon I moved back to more familiar territory: Washington, D.C. While I was working the Republic Gardens, Edgar Hayes, the bandleader, came in. He offered me a job as vocalist with his orchestra. What do you know, I was going to work in New York! The world was getting bigger and better every day.

We worked at the famous Savoy Ballroom, and Whitey's Lindy Hoppers were the showstoppers. What a crazy place that was: sitting on the bandstand with people passing by, looking at the vocalist, was almost too much to bear. We also played some one-nighters around, and then the Apollo Theatre. Oh! Honey, I can't write what went on inside this girl. No one can write emotions like this and make you really feel it.

Edgar Hayes broke up the band, but by now I could do a red-hot single, so I got bookings in the Club Bali (D.C.), Crystal Caverns (D.C.), and a few other places where I couldn't get in before. And, mind you, the salary was fifty dollars and tips. (They were still snatching it off the tables and by then I could really snatch.) Pottsville and places like that were passé. I was traveling fast now. While working at the Apollo doing a stint in front of the chorus, I was asked by the Sunset Royal Band to go along to Baltimore and Washington with them.

The first time I played the Royal in Baltimore, I rushed out front to see my name on the billboard after the first show. There was the name of the girl who had worked with them before. I was stung and angry, because I'd gotten a big hand inside and I wanted to see that billing right. Jonah, of the team Jonah and Foster, gave me good advice. I can be grateful for many things this man taught me. He passed by and listened to my ranting and raving for a moment, and then he said, "Go back in and keep doing the best shows you can. The audience's reaction will finally see that you get your billing."

Every show, I tried harder and harder, and about two days later, coming back from the restaurant across the street, I saw Mr. Jonah standing out front. He called me over and pointed his finger. There, bold as day, was a white piece of paper pasted over the other girl's name, and printed in big black letters was my name. Another lesson learned: just do the job and someone will have to see you someday, especially when God has already planned these things for you. Man has nothing to do but be beautiful. (But, Lord, he makes such a chore of it!)

From the Royal Theatre we went to the Howard Theatre in Washington, and two or three days after we opened we were asked to become a part of something no one wanted to believe could happen again: war. World War II broke out December 7th and we were in Camp Hood, Texas, by January 12th. Evelyn, a dancer, the band and I comprised the show, and the boys received us well. The camps weren't even set up for soldiers yet. We spent five weeks in Texas; then we crossed over a few states and reached the land of sunshine, California. Palm trees, cactus, and oranges, lemons, and grapefruits growing on trees—what a sight!

There were six of us on my second USO tour: Fetaque Saunders (a magician and the M.C.), Freddie and Flo (comedy, song and dance), a pianist named Basil Spears, Bobby Wallace doing imitations, and myself. Seldom were we mistreated, for if you were the camp would get no more entertainers. At one particular camp, though, Freddie could have lost his life because of a stupid blunder. They had assigned us to our rooms and we had started to unpack. Flo and I thought of some things we needed from the PX, so we left Freddie and took our walk. When we returned a crowd was outside the barracks. Some nut was screaming that there was a colored man in her place. They had mixed up the rooms in assigning them. She'd walked in, found poor Freddie washing his socks, and in no time at all she was a maniac. MPs were everywhere, and this innocent man, who had come to bring joy, could have been killed for no reason at all. Cute Freddie's not even five feet tall, with a heart soft as a marshmallow, and he had only gone to the room to which he had been assigned. Now came the highest insult of all. They calmed the screaming female, took the bed out, and sat it on the lawn—as if he had germs! We didn't feel like entertaining these people at all. In fact, we started not to—but I'm glad we did. Why should all the boys suffer for one ignorant person? However, I wouldn't say that we performed with spirit.

George Air Force Base had no place for us to stay. They were busy setting up a camp, so they took us to a place called Murray's Dude Ranch, a few miles from the base. Joe Louis later trained and had a cottage there, and many famous people visited the ranch. It was the only colored dude ranch in the country, Mr. Murray said. There was a great big swimming pool (Olympic size), a big restaurant, and all around the wall were clothespins hooked on a line with names of famous folk written on them. (Lots of Western pictures were made there.) We were three days at this place, but I was to see more of it later.

Fort Huachuca, Arizona, became our home for thirty days. There were so many soldiers there they made us a home-based troupe. We had a good time with the Ninety-second Division. Ralph, Baby-Face Ned, so many dear guys, mostly noncoms (and one dearer than the others). There were many charming brass, but as usual I went for (if you want to say underdog) a noncom.

On the twenty-ninth day a queer thing happened. The picture Stormy Weather had just been made, and we were to be honored by the presence of the stars, among them the beautiful Lena Horne. If memory serves me right, her uncle was entertainment director and he'd really set up a wonderful affair for the men. The Army newspaper said that Pearl Bailey would sing one song. Some of the troupe (including myself) felt it wasn't fair not to include us all, even if it was only in the finale, since we'd been there giving our all for a month. But the "powers" gave a firm no. After all, we were not the big shots. Two shows were set up—an inside one for the brass and an outdoor show for the enlisted men. The inside show went on first, and what a triumph it was. The fellows screamed and carried on ridiculously. My one song became three or four. After my stint came Babe Wallace singing and Miss Horne singing.

(Boy, was I glad I was through. It's never good to have too much of the same thing.)

There was quite a bit of discussion in the back room when the show was over, some of it pretty loud and angry. Of course, our little group was as pleased as punch. Over to the outdoor arena we went with hope in our hearts that Pearlie Mae, representing our troupe, would be the smash she'd been inside. However, we were in for a shock. The order of the show had undergone a change; everyone went on before me and I got scared. By the time the boys sat through that long show, I knew I wouldn't be the same hit. On and on it went and then my name was called; so with quaking knees I started to the front of the stage and God put His loving arms around me; the heavens opened and rain came down like you could never believe. The soldiers scattered like flies. Dear God, thank you.

Later, some boys showed us a pitcure that supposedly had been taken while the show was on inside, and it was weird. Though Lena and I were never on the stage together, there we were apparently standing side by side onstage. The photographer had faked it. We are dear friends now and stand on the stage together knowing it. Sister Lena, Fate was speaking to us.

The last stop was California again, and in L.A. I left the group. Herb Jeffries, who used to work with Duke Ellington, and made the song "Flamingo" popular, had a club called the Flamingo. He offered me a job singing there (not too much money). I lived at the Morris Hotel on Fifth Street. Funny thing, one side of the street was class; on the other side the winos hung out. If you went over there, you could get into trouble, but strangely enough they never came on our side. Poor Avery Parrish (the pianist who made the famous recording of the "After Hours" blues with Erskine Hawkins) wandered over to the wrong side one night, was hit on the head with a bar stool, and never recovered. Such a beautiful musician, too!

A romance blossomed there for me and continued for some time seriously, which I must say I should have avoided. Youth and inexperience are so helpless and sad.

Fats Waller, that master, used to come by Herb's

Flamingo and play the piano and sing for his own pleasure. He'd let me sit on the floor (it was only a small platform stage) and ad-lib some of the songs with him. He taught me the words to his latest songs from *Early to Bed*. One was "There's a Man in My Life." We missed him a few nights, and when he showed up again he was so pale; he'd had influenza. Next job for him was the Greenwich Village Inn, New York, but he seemed worried about the fact that the weather was so cold there. Around December 18th, dear Fats was headed for New York and died on the train. The world lost a great (and the word fits here) artist.

Later, I joined Cootie Williams' band. An original Ellington man, Cootie had a great influence on my getting together a basic act. He never called me for one song; I sat on that cotton-picking bandstand till I wanted to cry, waiting my turn. Then he would call me to do about six numbers at once (no dancing). Everyone else wanted me to throw in that fast buck dance, but then I thought of myself as strictly a vocalist. The arrangements by The Master, Don Redman, were the nicest thing. From the beginning Don knew how to write the proper background for me and, for that matter, for most performers.

Around then, the time came for me to have an agent, and I went to a man named Nat Nazarro. He had been a great performer himself and handled Bill at that time, the Berry Brothers, Moke and Poke, Stump and Stumpy, and was the man who brought Buck and Bubbles into prominence.

Not long after, I had one of my first setbacks in show business. Helen Humes left Count Basie and I got a call to replace her. Basie's band was so well known that my heart stopped at the thought of singing with them. We went up to Worcester, Mass., and I sang and they made me do a dance. Well, my option wasn't picked up—and my heart was broken!

Recently I had a chance to tell Basie (a darling man) what I did then. I called his manager, or the gentleman I thought was his manager. I couldn't get through at first, but I kept trying, and finally this man must have gotten sick of his secretary being bothered, so he picked up the call.

I asked him to give me another chance to prove myself—
without the dance. I thought I could satisfy. This man
told me in no uncertain terms I did not have the ability
and wouldn't fit. This was my first real hurt in our business.
Today, bless his heart, this man is one of my biggest fans.
He's often run into me, and he rates me among the greatest.
I don't think he even remembers that incident. Dear man,
I don't mind now, because you had every right to your
opinion. The only thing that really hurt was the way you
said it. It was ugly, but it paid off. I tried harder.

Max Gordon, owner of the Village Vanguard, was another helpful person to me. When I got a job at the Vanguard, he let me have complete freedom of expression in
delivery. The USO had helped me a lot; those soldiers
really wanted lots of entertainment. You sang and talked
and joked, so I'd really developed more talents than I
dreamed of. Eddie Heywood was the pianist, Keg Johnson
the drummer. The bass player's name escapes me now, but,
friend, I appreciate your help. We practically made it all
up as we went, and I stayed there some time. The first
time at the Vanguard I worked with the unbelievable
Huddie Ledbetter. (He was the blues singer who was once
on a chain gang.) And I also worked with Richard Dyer-
Bennet there. It was a different crowd that came to the
club: artistic people, society, a strange mixture. You really
were truly judged here. My work was poker-faced, and
folks thought that was a style. It wasn't. I had large gaps
in my teeth, and that's why I didn't smile much. I just
kept that "pussycat" smile for years. Now that Doc Shapiro
has fixed my teeth, baby, no one, but no one, can open up
like Pearlie Mae.

The Ink Spots were one of the biggest drawing cards
during the forties. People would line up for blocks to hear
them, and though they had many sensational hits, "If I
Didn't Care" was the moneymaker. Bill Kenny, Deek Wat-
son, Hoppy Jones, and Charlie Fuqua had something going
for them. Came the opportunity to do a few weeks with
them. Actually, I was hired as a "time waster," I think
(and because they used the Sunset Royal Band a lot, and
I was with them then). The Ink Spots did seven to nine

shows a day, and they really cleaned up. Naturally, when they had to do so many shows, the rest of the acts were cut short. In fact, we weren't needed, for folks wanted only to see and hear them. Of course, it had no bearing on our salary. But I wanted to be seen and heard, so it bothered me. Coming off one day at the Palace Theatre in Akron, Ohio, after singing my two selections, I expressed my unhappiness at the audience's reaction. They enjoyed my songs, but the hand was not what I thought it should have been, and I was blaming the musicians, the audience, everybody but Pearlie Mae.

That comedy team, Jonah and Foster, was on the bill. Mr. Jonah, as I've said, had quite a few tidbits of good advice to give me throughout my show-business career. He's gone now, but I've never forgotten his words of wisdom. He came to the wings and listened to my carrying on for a few moments. Then I got told off.

He said, "And how did you do, young lady?"

I turned to him and answered, "Well, I—" and that's as far as I got, because he said then, "Did you do your best? Or were you too busy listening to the errors of the band to do your best?"

I had to stop and think what had really happened, and when I started to answer he had gone and left me standing alone with my miserable self. That was the end of that sort of thing for me in show business. Today I think the musicians have as high a regard for me as I have for them.

At the height of their fame, Hoppy (that wonderful bass sound) died, and the Spots seemed to start breaking up. Not that they weren't still popular and making money, but soon they were having court battles, and later on they did split up permanently. Each one got a Spot going for himself, and even today heaven only knows how many Ink Spots there are running around. (Wonder what all the civil-rights groups think of that name now? Should it be "The Black Spots"—what about the other color inks?)

Well, Pearlie was rolling. Looking back, I can see how really rough it was sometimes. I had worked in all sorts of places, and there were disappointments, but I still had a pride in myself and what I was doing, and a feeling for

humanity that all the hard times couldn't knock out of me.
An expression of it follows:

TO HUMANITY

Do you find the road you travel rough
And the going hard and slow?
I traveled the selfsame road, my friend,
A long, long time ago.
Are you disappointed, tired and hurt
And a bit too proud to cry,
And so brush the tears away with a smile?
Shake, buddy, so do I.

3

In July of 1944, my manager then, Chauncey Olman, got me a trial at the Blue Angel on the Upper East Side of New York. Now, let me tell you, that's saying something. If you don't know New York, or didn't in the forties, you can't understand what it meant to be on that side of town. That's where the society big shots and the finest stores were, and still remain largely. Of course, there are a few strange birds over there, but they're quality, too.

The club was run by a man from France, Herbert Jacoby. Later on, my old boss from the Vanguard, Max Gordon, was there, too. Jacoby came in every afternoon to see that the flowers in the tall vase on the piano were just right, and he always wore black suits. I used to tell him he looked more like an undertaker than a nightclub owner. The Herman Chitterson trio played for all the acts (there were only three or four), and we went on at half-hour intervals. Evelyn Knight, Professor Corey, George and Bert Bernard, Maxine Sullivan, Portia Nelson—many of us worked there for months at a time.

It was a delicious job, class all the way. Only the best

clientele came: Grace Moore, Garbo, Jimmy Donahue, Libby Holman, Dietrich. What a name dropper I was becoming! I had read about these people but had never seen them. But only once did anyone come in that *everyone* really stared at, and that was Garbo. This woman's face is not to be believed, and if ever there was a legend, she's it.

The Blue Angel was a small place, seating only about two hundred, and Herb had those tiny tables so close together you practically were sitting in someone's lap. But no one cared; some may even have come for that purpose. (Oh, Pearl, that mind of yours!)

The trial engagement ended and I went through the summer with other little jobs. Then the first week in September, Chauncey called to say Jacoby had picked up the option and I was to return for four weeks with options. This time around I met more famous personalities, and one lady really struck me as wonderful. One night I went to the bar to have a cold beer (my drink by now; I still haven't to this day had whiskey or strong wine). How I loved beer! I was in a big hurry to get one, and not being able to attract the bartender's attention, I did something that I now detest people to do to me. I popped my fingers. As I made this dramatic and rude gesture, a deep voice said, "Don't do that, darling. It's rude." I looked up at the sound of this quiet but powerful voice, and there sat the tiniest lady on the next stool. We started to talk. She said she enjoyed my act and introduced herself: Miss Polly Adler of *A House Is Not a Home* fame. In case you're not an avid reader, or the name escapes you, Miss Adler was the famous sporting-house madam. She told me her name meant "Pearl" in Polish.

For years thereafter we ran into each other, at Ciro's and the Mocambo in Hollywood and other places, and became fast friends. This lady told me that she never had a chance to get much schooling and she wanted an education. And, folks, she did return to school, got A's on her report card, and graduated with a B.A. degree. So all of you who keep screaming it's too late or you're too old to get an education, shame on you!

Anyway, I had this job at the Angel, but I didn't have

the clothes to go with it. I solved this by going around the corner from the Braddock Hotel on 126th Street and Eighth Avenue, where I lived, to the thrift shop. They had wedding gowns there, beautiful lace with long sleeves (and that I appreciated, because I didn't like the naked look) that cost about fifteen bucks. I'd have the trains cut off and be in business. All in all, I had three dresses.

Two gentlemen used to come into the club practically every night (it was a happy place that folks liked to come back to), and they would send for me to chat with them. They talked about art, books, and the cultures of the world, which awed me. I loved listening to them, and I think they liked listening to me (I was a philosopher from way back!)—you know, you teach and you learn. The surprise of my life came one night when they told me to go to (wow!) Lord and Taylor's and get myself a dress. I didn't take from men, but these two were certainly not wanting to take anything from me, and I wasn't so nutty as to think it was romantic interest. I'd never been inside Lord and Taylor's, though I'd slowly walked by many times at night on my way home from the club. During those years it was lovely to walk down the streets of New York, and window-shop at 3 or 4 A.M. Try it now, even at three or four in the afternoon, and you may not make it. (Or, for that matter, in any city in America now—shame!) You're afraid to leave your hotel room for a sandwich after work, and the bellman is afraid to go for you. But then: oh, happy days, how glad I am I had a chance to be part of you then, New York. A green long-sleeved number was my choice, very plain, and it cost sixty-nine smackers. That was close to what I made a week. That night when they came in I was decked out, and they approved of my taste in clothes. Needless to say, it was worn often, and thank you, guys, very much for the frock.

Option after option was picked up. After eight months, I was still an Angel fixture. My name was getting mentioned in theatrical circles: "Go over to the Angel and see that new girl." Time was being good to me and Fate was getting ready to smack me in the face with a goodie.

Love-life things were going wrong (again). He had an

act which was very successful (it was even before he joined it) and, oh, was he evermore being a star! I can say that and mean it, because by this time I'd heeded the advice of my elders in the business and had both feet firmly planted on the ground, from which even to this day they have not moved. There was no hat to fit his head, and he went strutting like a peacock. Such a nice person in most other ways, too. But this attitude of his led to continuous clashes between us, and though my job was good, he wanted me to know that I was not in his class.

One day, feeling very down, I went for a rare visit to his partner's house. He was getting sick of him, too; it was his partner's original act, yet he was getting told off. His wife and he treated me kindly, and after a short time I started down the street, melancholy but with hope we'd make it. At the hotel there were quite a few messages marked "Urgent" from Chauncey and the William Morris Agency, with whom I had never had any direct connection. On calling Chauncey, I received word to get down immediately to the Strand Theatre; Sister Rosetta Thorpe had a strep throat and couldn't go on that night. She was a dynamic entertainer and was playing on the bill with (hold your hats) the great Cab Calloway. She had "Extra Added Attraction" billing because she was a fine act, too. Swinging the spirituals and playing her guitar, she'd rock an audience.

Arriving at the theatre, I was sent upstairs to the rehearsal hall and there stood the Mighty Calloway. I had seen him onstage but never close up. He was a handsome man, with gorgeous hair, and so alive-looking. He said not a word, and the fellow with the band took my three-piece arrangements. (This was all I had, except my specialty "St. Louis Blues," which no one did fast like me, and "Tired." At the club the trio and I made up most of the other stuff, because my other jobs had been either with bands that kept their music when I left or small groups you just hummed your arrangement to.) Anyhow, I had a short, fifteen-minute rehearsal, with the men staring at me and probably wondering what was going to happen on the stage that night.

I was to sing four numbers, including (if I got my encore)

"Fifteen Years," "Straighten Up and Fly Right," "Tired," and "St. Louis Blues." Chauncey got Jacoby's permission to let me go over to the Strand and do the ten o'clock show and return to the Angel. I didn't go on there until ten, anyhow. He was reluctant. (But thank you, doll, for not taking the opportunity away.)

It was a shaky Pearl who entered the portals of the Strand that night. My manager, these strange men from William Morris, and the manager of the theatre, Mr. Harry Meyer (a sweetie pie), watched from afar as I went out on that great big stage with all those people jammed in that place. I remember Cab leaning on the far side of the stage watching (it was his show and he could have no junk out there). I did my numbers, and then I heard something that perhaps I'd never hear again (I have, thank God, but it will never again sound just like that to me). It was applause, real. Thunder, lightning, and all the elements spoke at once.

The next thing I knew, I was walking to the far corner backstage and someone said, "Where are you going?" and I said, "Over to that corner to pray."

No one came near me in that corner; they watched, but maybe they realized something bigger than all of them was in the corner with me, and they knew better than to draw near. Many performers had heard the news uptown that Bill's sister was to go on for Thorpe, and had caught the show. When I finished my stint at the Angel that night and got back uptown, the news had spread like wildfire, and to them I was already a star.

Harlem was talking, and even my "love life" made the grand decision that I was now in his league, so while we celebrated that night he told me how stars should act. Me, I wanted still to be Pearl; but no, he said, "You got 'em where you want 'em, so kick 'em in the butt." Sorry, mister, I had to disappoint you. Even then my feet hurt too bad to kick my fellow man. "Lover Boy" later in my career sent me an orchid backstage (and I hate corsages) with a note staying, "When you are big, act big." Not caring to resume our relationship and not liking to wear flowers (which he knew), I responded, "When you're big, you don't have to act at all. . . ."

Sister Thorpe appeared on the scene the next morning before the first show and said she could make it, but Mr. Calloway had other ideas. He told her to rest her throat for a few days. She did, and after four days she returned. By this time, Cab had decided not to pick up her option, and took me instead to his next dates, three weeks of theatres, and then had us booked into the famous Zanzibar on Broadway for sixteen weeks.

All right, Pearlie Mae, you could start to believe at last that Pottsville had paid off. My brother Bill was to be the other headliner on the show. Our dream had come true: we were in show biz together: the Baileys of Virginia had two artists in the family. Chauncey had set a deal for me to get six hundred dollars in real American money, plus transportation. First-class hotels, cities I'd only read of in geography books, rooms with bath, and "Extra Added Attraction" billing. That girl who had stood in front of a theatre griping because she couldn't see the billing was now able to read it from across the street. The reviews were great for me every place we played, but Cab never said a word to me. He very seldom spoke to anyone around him on the show, but he was very nice to me—a nod here and there. He was one of the biggest draws of his time, and he really packed the theatres. Later, I could realize the terrific job he had running an organization; he couldn't afford any wasted time or effort.

Dottie Saulters was Cab's band vocalist (little Dottie from the Kiddie Hour in Philly) and we had a ball. Poor sweet Dot is gone now; she left us so young.

I remember on that tour we played Canton, Ohio. Little Dottie Saulters and I stayed in the hotel, and the band boys lived around the town. Well, at that time in Canton all races weren't welcome in certain hotels. One night I made a long-distance call to the boy friend, and in the background of our conversation this little dry voice kept cutting in with these insulting words. That little voice was saying dirty things—like it was putting us on. I checked with the long-distance operator and she said, "I hear it, too." I found out later it was the lady down at the switchboard who was doing this. The supervisor checked and found it was coming from right downstairs in the hotel. Well, the manager got ahold of this thing, and they really got on to this woman.

Anyhow, speaking about people who can make mistakes by getting the wrong chip on their shoulder, that was me. I came downstairs after the call. And when I walked out of the hotel toward the theatre right across the street, there was a nice young man and lady standing against the building. And as I walked by they looked at me. And they looked at me hard, but I kept walking. And now I was burning, see, because of this thing that had happened on the phone.

So I stood there for a moment and these people just kept staring. Then I started across the street to the theatre, and they were still looking hard. As I got to the corner I turned around and said, "What are you looking at?" in a mean voice, because I was angry. And this man said, "We're just looking at you. My wife saw the show last night, and we were just admiring you."

Well, I tell you, I was so ashamed. I stood and explained the story of my life to these people. And the more I explained, the sillier I felt, because I was explaining what happened in the hotel and the whole thing. So when I finally did cross the street, all I could do was keep looking back and waving my hand, you know, in a friendly gesture. I think twice in my life that sort of thing has happened to me. When you think about it, you start to realize everyone's not really looking at you for the reasons you might think.

Came the debut at the Zanzibar, and by now everybody turned out to see this new comet who had crossed the sky of the theatre. The comet was scared, but ready to do her best. The critics and the public accepted me; and when that happens in our world, then your work has just begun! Brother Willie beamed, although my reviews were equal to his and Cab's. (Remember, those two drew them in; if their names had not been out front, no one would have seen me inside.) Mr. Howard, the owner, said, "Pearl, this is a wonderful time to achieve success. There's a war on,

and to be able to make folks stand up and notice you at
this time means you've got something." Bill Robinson, the
greatest tap dancer in the world, came in one night and
spoke with me. Something he said will go to my grave with
me. He said, "Little girl, you don't know what you have,
and I hope you never find out." Uncle Bo, whatever it is I
hope I don't find out, either, because I may misuse it and
that would be sad. I might hurt someone or become a different human being.

We did many benefits, sometimes three a night plus
three shows, but the excitement kept telling me I could
take it (how it lied). I went to the prizefights between
shows, saw the greatest and nicest man in this universe,
the real champ, Joe Louis, and Sugar Ray Robinson
(best all-round fighter), Henry Armstrong (three-division
champ), and Rocky Graziano. I went to ball games, did
all the delightful things I'd heard about. The gravy train
was rolling and I was riding on it. We'd walk uptown nights
(at least most of the way) to Creole Pete's, Jenny Lou's,
and hang out till four o'clock closing time at Beefsteak
Charlie's. Beer (draft) was ten cents, and how we guzzled
it, plus the free snacks. Lionel Hampton, Cook and Brown,
Sweetpea (Billy Strayhorn), Theresa (checkroom lady from
the Latin Quarter)—all the musicians and entertainers were
there! It was a gas.

Only one thing was wrong at the club. It shouldn't have
mattered, but it did. Since I loved people, it bugged me
not to be friendly with everyone. The Zanzibar had a line
of lovely girls known as "The Zanzibeauts," and they
literally took that to heart. We all dressed on the same
floor and had to pass each other all night, but they were
such a clan that they never spoke. I wanted to be friends
so badly, but it was all in vain. They wouldn't hang out in
Beefsteak's; they hung out next door where the more "in"
and "money" crowd went. I guess they'd been at the club
so long they were sure of their jobs. Little did they know
that the time would come when a chorus girl could hardly
get a job.

Then came that night, that rare and wonderful night
Fate arranged a way for me to become one of the girls, a

member of the clan. There was a young, exciting man on the horizon who had the world in a dither. His name was Frank Sinatra. He paid a visit to the club, and after the show a waiter came to the dressing room and said, "Mr. Sinatra would like to come up and tell you how much he enjoyed your work." My darling colleagues heard the news and dashed into my tiny dressing room to ask if they could meet him. There was a small hallway you had to come around to get to Cab's or my room, but at the head of the stairs was a room for the girls. (That's why later on it was so cute to hear them explain that they had never spoken because they couldn't see me when I came to work.)

When he arrived, I asked him if he would stand at the door of the girls' room. They wanted to trace around his feet so everyone would know Sinatra stood there. He obliged, and they took fingernail polish and made the drawing. Frankie, doll, you got me accepted by the girls, but after I was in there I still didn't hang out with them at all. They were too hip for me. Beefsteak's still had the coldest beer and the dearest friends.

Frank came again and said he wanted me to do a record with him. He needed it like a hole in his head, but we did it. It was called "A Little Learning Is a Dangerous Thing." Funny, Frank, that record never became popular, and I think I know the reason. It's because you and I made some pretty smart ad libs on there, and I think at that time we were either too far ahead of the people or too far ahead of ourselves.

Frank always had to leave the club by the back door; the mob would have torn him apart. Boy, I was swollen with pride at this man's being interested in my work. I told him so one time, and he laughs about it now. Boy, the bobby soxers were swooning over him and I must confess that with silk stockings I was falling on my face, too. He always looked so helpless and was so skinny; I think every female wanted to mother him. He probably could have had more "mothers" and "lovers" at one time than any other man in history. Frankie, your friendship I've treasured through the years; your goodness to your fellow man I've admired. People don't hear of the nice things this man does. When someone is in need, he's one of the first there. How do you know, Pearl? Never mind, I do.

Not too long before when he "returned" and made *From Here to Eternity,* he opened at the Latin Quarter in Boston. Frank, I sat in the back of the room and the place was not full, but you sang your heart out; things weren't that big for you then. Later we rode over to see my husband Louie, who was playing with Duke at Storyville, and though you said nothing, you seemed so lost and lonely. It's phenomenal that a man who was so big in the profession, then slipped down, has risen above it all again. Some of his experience may have left him bitter. Who knows the insides of any man? But the last time I looked into his face, I saw the will of a man to do what would make him and others happy. You're a strong person, Frank. Don't look back, only forward—for you've seen both ends of the road and know now a man can only travel one way: straight through with happiness. And I still swoon when I see you work.

The next time I played the Zanzibar for a long engagement (in 1946), I became absolutely exhausted and had to have a few days off. I came on the stage one night, grabbed Cab's arm without realizing it, and held on for dear life for the whole act. Singing "Tired" was no lie. Mr. Howard advised time off, and darling Manny Sachs, the man who put me on Columbia Records, spoke of a doctor in Philly. Doc took one look at this tired female, got out the hammer, and started tapping my knees. I wondered if he thought I was some kind of nut. (I'd never been to such a fancy doctor before.)

"What do you do in the show?" he asked.

I named the songs and recited some of the lyrics. "Tired" was the one he seemed interested in, so I drawled out the words, "Tired of the life I lead,/Tired of the blues I breed,/Tired counting things I need . . ."

He stopped me with, "Lady, please. I'm getting tired just listening to you." He told me to go back to work but not to sing that song for a few days; mentally and physically, I was so fatigued, and the more I said these words the more I convinced myself that I was really tired.

I understood him, and I did what he said. He was right. I started to feel better and soon was crooning as usual.

Atlantic City was another spot I worked then. The Yacht Club had once been one of the most famous places in the country, but was now on its last legs. I lived with an elderly lady named Mrs. Thompson, on Kentucky Avenue. We would sit in her kitchen and chat away. I love older people, especially those who've grown wiser and more beautiful. Some folks have never been happy, and when they grow older they're miserable to themselves and all around them. They scream, "It's because I'm old that I'm being mistreated." I'd like to say a few words to these old folks: No, love, it's because you've forgotten to pick up the things God gave you that others deny you the pleasure of getting the love you seek. It's still there, if you'd only seek it and stop thinking the world owes it to you.

This applies to everyone, too, not just unhappy old people. Love comes to the lovable—the loving—at any stage of life.

4

Loving is so important to me, particularly needing to be loved.

My first marriage way back when I was a kid on the coal circuit in the thirties was one try to find love. That was so long ago it doesn't even seem real now. He was a drummer, and we only were married about eighteen months.

In 1948 there was a thing going that had started back at Fort Huachuca, and it so real that eventually we were married. This was a person that I can say nothing but the best about; he was a warm man. I think our marriage went wrong because he came back from the war like many men, unable to adjust to the situations that had changed while he was overseas. He had been slightly wounded, so got a pension. Unfortunately, he sat on it, the pension and all. Every day there'd be a knock on our door, bam, bam, bam. Some of the boys would be standing there with a fifth, you know. I would get two big Smithfield hams for thirteen dollars apiece for meals and they would be gone in one day. So, you know, I didn't want these people. I'm in show business, but you know I never ran a liquor house.

And I wasn't used to people coming in and sitting around the house all day juicing up. That's not what my mother raised me to get into. There was a resentment that I never liked his friends, but I said, "Listen, let me tell you. I don't care what you do, I don't care what you drink, but if I *invite* someone to my house, and I know that he is a drinker, *I* will have something to drink in there for him. I don't want him, in broad daylight, ringing the bell with the neighbors looking around, bringing a fifth of whiskey to just sit around with a bunch of guys and just talk all day." The Washington socialites, you see, would come around and sit all day and party in the house. I guess they thought this was how theatrical people lived. So it didn't go, with that. It just didn't jell.

His ability to *do* was too great just to lie around, and that's what went wrong. I gave up the whole scene. Today we're very good friends, and we understand that we live different ways and it wouldn't have worked out. I have a deep respect for the gentleman, and I know he has for me. How strange that the man we got to sell our home should have turned out to be my nemesis!

I will call him Jim. He was a good-looking, brilliant, wealthy Washington playboy. The wealth was from his family's real estate business. The girls just fainted at the sight of him.

When I speak of the unhappy life, I think mostly of my marriage to him in Washington. I will tell about it because it has had a meaning in my life, but I must be careful not to hurt those who were involved. Word has come to me that he died several years ago, but I suppose by saying things and telling names, I could hurt those who loved him. That I do not want.

I had heard of Jim by reputation. Actually, as it turned out, my first feelings about him were right. He had run into my husband somewhere and asked us both out for a big party on his boat. And I said to my husband, "I don't want to go on a boat with those people," because first of all they really boozed it up. They really had a ball at their parties. I said, "I don't want to because I don't know him." But I'd heard about him and his boat, and the girls and everything. My husband didn't even particularly like him, but he wanted to be accepted in his company. I didn't much like that group because it was mostly a whole lot of girls. I was thinking that once me and my husband got into that kind of setup—in there with all those girls—I could be getting my own marriage in trouble. So it ended up that I didn't go.

Well, when I broke up with my husband I was at the Blue Angel, and a guy came up one night, and he had a girl with him. Lo and behold—Jim. And the funniest thing, it happens that this same young girl would be important later, but I didn't know it then. I drove my car back to Washington that night I finished, and they waited and came back when I did. I was going back to make a deal to sell the house I had then on Irving Street. I sold it to a doctor. In fact, I almost gave it away. Jim was a friend of the doctor's and he handled everything. And in the correspondence about the real estate, we became friends.

But I was right the first time when I said I did not want to go on that boat. Was I evermore right! Everybody in Washington said, "Oh boy, this is going to be a shame because she doesn't know him." But this man was brilliant and handsome. His son (I'll call him Robby) is still like my own son; he has the deepest regard for me, extremely deep. Robby was ranked thirteenth when he was at the University of Heidelberg. (He was studying Russian.) He's now a captain in the Air Force, thirty-three years old.

That marriage is hard to tell about even now. Once I told Angie, my sax player, that it was like there's a wall, and I've been bracing the wall up to keep it from toppling over; and all of a sudden I've taken away the braces, mentally and physically. The braces that I had there I didn't need anymore. The wall was standing by itself, even though I thought it was falling. Sometimes you think the whole world is falling, and it's only yourself that's leaning. The wall is always straight. It's like the Great Wall of China, going around more than a city; it's going around a lot of people and a lot of hearts. Yet people can go over it, and someday somebody digs under it. As you grow you'll cross over that wall and say, "I am crossing the place where a wall used to be." And then one day you'll grow and say, "I *think* there was a wall here once." And then you'll say, "I always thought there was a wall here, but, you know, there never was a real wall. I imagined it." You have come to a point where you know that you could have walked through that big brick wall. If your thought and belief and faith become that strong, then you can smile about it. You'll say, "I could have walked completely through that brick wall because it never really was there. I *put* it there."

From the friendship over the real estate business came the marriage. I started to see it was a bad thing almost immediately. Jim was still the same playboy. Maybe in a way it was also not a good thing for Jim to be married to a wife well known in show business. It has happened with many couples that the husband starts sort of drifting toward being a part of that world too much.

I don't think any man sets out to quit his job, but we have a very fascinating business. The husband may come up to see his wife at the cabaret for the weekend. He gets engrossed, and it's a different world. It's also different money, and a lot of these fellows decide, "Listen, a married couple wants to be together; what could I take care of for you?" Some get the idea they want to be managers, which never was Jim's case. Then some of them start skipping days of their own work, because, what the heck, somebody else is working in the family. And their work seems dull beside this glamour. There are many people outside the business who see the inside of it and are attracted; it offers them a life which they could never have for themselves. Besides the financial attractions they are fascinated by the crowd and the excitement. This can turn out bad.

While Jim and I were married, I had a house in Washington, on Channing Street, and I was working at La Directoire in New York. I would commute from Washington, D.C., to New York City every day at first, because when my feelings for anyone are strong, they're really strong. I'd finish at two, catch the milk train, which got me in to Washington at 8 A.M. only to go to bed, not *with* anyone, because actually he was at work or just "out." But I hoped I would be with him at least for the few hours. That's important to me when I like people. And then I would catch the four o'clock afternoon train and get back at eight for my show. Some nights I would fly if I could get out there and catch a freight plane. I've sat on a plane when I was the only passenger.

I'd call Jim before I left New York and say, "I'm coming in." He'd say, "Oh, great! I'll meet you at the airport." And I would get there and just stand there, stupid. No one. I've gone and kneeled at a window of the house and just looked out, and the tears would be coming, and I would wonder, "Where is he?" I probably knew but didn't want to believe.

Once I came in to Washington airport, at night—there was nobody. So, next day, time to go back. I went to get the plane, and one of the porters said to me, "Gee, you folks really travel a lot." I said, "Oh, yes, I'm going back," and before I could say, "to New York to work," he said, "Gee, because your husband was just through here; he was going to Dallas. Are you going to Dallas, too?" I said, "Oh, no, I'm going to New York." And it's a wild thing to hear that your husband is going to Dallas when you're catching a plane going the other direction. I knew he had a girl there. I had some moments that were heartbreaking. (Now I have to smile, because I enjoy my present husband much more for having had such an opposite kind of experience in the past.)

Actually, it wasn't too much better when Jim and I were together. Once some big numbers backer was giving a big party. Usually I didn't go to these things, but this man happened to be pretty nice. Jim said, "Come on and go," and I said okay. I got in the car, and there was a pack of cigarettes—and I'll never forget it was a red package, Virginia Rounds or something—fastened with a rubber band onto my car mirror. I said, "I don't smoke those," and he said, "Of course not, my girl does." In the trunk of the car there was a bathing suit, the sand from the beach and everything, and I thought, "Oh boy, am I kidding?"

The party was out in Maryland, a crab feast. I sat playing cards and watching him getting drunker and drunker. Suddenly, about six o'clock, he says, "Give me the keys." It had started to rain outside, so everybody was inside. "Give me the keys."

"What keys?"

"The keys to your car, because I got a date in town."

Everybody was listening. Now, one thing I always told him, "Everybody in Washington knows you. And they expect you to insult me. Out of town you can insult me, but never do it in this one town, Washington. I'm going to live with whatever you do, but don't insult me publicly in Washington."

Whatever anybody said never mattered to me as long as his behavior never came out publicly in that town. I just didn't want it to happen there. Actually, it was partly to save him, because everybody said he was that kind of guy. I was trying to get him to show them it wasn't true.

I said, "Oh no, I can't give you the car keys." And I just walked out, to get me a can of beer. Now the rain which had moved us inside stopped, and everybody—all the numbers backers, the socialites, the big shots—came out to get a little beer. And Jim started calling me names. I think he called me plus the people everything in the book. You didn't have to do anything for him to do this. When he got drunk, he was the kind of person who would just insult his mother or anybody. He started in on me. I remember one of the men said, "This is *your* wife, but if you call this lady another name, I'm going to do something about it." Now, the fellow that said it was some big numbers man. I don't even remember who it was. I was well liked in that town, and Jim wasn't about to answer him. In a respect it was my home, too. And actually Jim wasn't liked, particularly by men, because he had gone a bit too far with so many of their wives and girl friends.

I just stood there—I'm a person of emotions, too—but for once I didn't get angry. I could have thrown a beer can at him or done something like that, but I was just watching him. As he called these names, I was just standing there looking at him. I thought, "What is this? There's no connection here with my thinking about living." Somehow I wanted to try to talk to him. But when this fellow spoke to him, Jim wandered away like he was just so drunk, and I said to the people, "Why don't you all go in and have a nice time. Don't worry." And they started to drift in, feeling, Well, she's getting embarrassed. Jim went around to the front porch, got up in a hammock, and he just suddenly conked out to sleep. A few of them came around, saying, "Come on, Jim, get up," and he got up out of the hammock, went down the stairs, and fell on the ground, out cold. And I still had the car keys. While he was lying there, I said, "Oh, he'll lie there, he'll be sober, don't worry; just don't worry. So he'll *catch* a cold." A couple of them just didn't go in, I think, because they wanted to stay there in case he got up and was nasty. They weren't going to let him go any further because it was just so cruel.

And you know what was in my mind that night? If they had gone in, I might have killed him, with no anger at all. I was thinking as he was lying on this ground soft from rain. I was like somebody in a dream, thinking here's a human being who is going to hurt his mother, his son, and everything he touches. And wouldn't it be nice, while he's lying there and the earth is soft, just to get in the car and just go back and forth, back and forth, just mash him down into the earth. There would be no cost for the burial at all. Just give him a nice place to rest, and then he couldn't hurt anybody else anymore. Without any anger, and I say that from the bottom of my heart, with no malice at all, I just wanted to do that one thing. He could never hurt anyone else anymore. It was just that this wonderful person, who I thought had all these potentials, had done nothing but hurt. Let us stop the agony. But I got in the car and left. He got up and somebody else took him home.

I remember once in 1950 we were staying in a New York hotel when a girl stopped by to visit that I'd met in London in 1948. I used to call her "The Duchess." Jim was a stranger to her, and he came in just loaded. Whenever he walked in drunk like that, he'd just start off on some subject in a very nasty way. He said, "Who's this cute bitch?" and I said, "Don't say that." He just said, "Aw, God," and went on insulting her. He was really something. One word led to another and I can remember this girl saying, "Pearl, he doesn't want you." I said to her, "You mustn't say that," and she said, "Accept it." Well, I went out of there. I was just sick.

One day I was sitting outside the house on Channing Street, and I knew it was ending. I was sitting on the front steps, and if it's ESP or whatever it is, I decided to go to a phone and dial a number I saw in our address book—listed as "music store in Dallas" (and he was no musician, believe me)—and I went around the corner to this drugstore and called the number. I didn't feel like I was snooping; it was just like a message to do this, I just knew, and I asked for the girl by name. "No," they said, "she's been in Washington. She's back at school now at Howard University and she's living in the dormitory." I said, "That's wonderful." I got in the car, still had just a house dress on, and I went to his parents' house. Remember, this was a very prominent family. His mother and father were sitting on the porch. She was a gorgeous woman (and I'll talk more about her later). I said, "At this time I could, if I wanted to, take a gun, go around to the dormitory and kill your son, kill the girl, and probably get off for second or third degree. But I like you two too much. Just tell me the best lawyer in town, and let's call it a day."

I went to the lawyer and explained the situation. He knew Jim; he'd even taught him some in law school. (Jim wasn't a lawyer, but he was a person who dug into everything.) The lawyer called Jim into the office and told him I wanted a divorce. Jim said, "She probably wants the house, and she can have it." The lawyer said, "She doesn't want anything but a divorce. Just go, just leave her alone."

Well, it turned out that the house had been put in my name—with all the mortgages. Also, Jim—who had lost his license, driving drunk, tickets, et cetera—and his friend had gone over into Virginia and traded my car in on another new Cadillac, which was in my name—this was already a federal case. But none of that business bothered me. I went back to New York to rehearse *Bless You All* and planned to come to Washington on my day off. Jim said, "Oh, I'll get me a fine apartment and everything, and my girl. Great!" By then it didn't mean a thing to me. The decision was made. I had nobody else in mind. It was just goodbye. It was an accepted fact.

But on Sunday I came back, and, oh, it was just wonderful. I cooked some food and we stayed there at home. He was still in there, but I'd asked him to take the other room until he found a place, since our relationship was severed. Yet I was hopeful. Then he moved to his apartment, and I said, "Have anything you want." I had all these extra linens and things stored in the basement, so I said, "Look, you're moving into an apartment tonight, you'll need things. Take anything you want." I watched him getting ready to go, and at one point as Jim came out of the basement, I saw a tear. Suddenly when the moving van came for his things, I saw something there: a lost human, or someone acting a role. Which one I don't know.

I came home the following Sunday on my day off. He said, "Have dinner with me." He could be a charming person, and by then he was almost like a brother to me. Nothing was there, and I knew it. I enjoyed that dinner with him.

And then the next week I came back late Saturday night, and I'll never forget it. I brought a lovely blue dress down, and I was so happy I was going to see him. I was wondering if maybe the move had made this person straighten out. And I truly liked him very much. But when I got there he was back in the house, very, very loaded up in the bed. This was about 5 or 6 A.M. A lady was helping me, and my niece from Washington happened to ride down from New York with me in the car, so they were in the house, too. I was upstairs hanging up this dress, and all of a sudden he says, "Aw, I don't want you." I said, "Great, you don't want me," because now it didn't even matter. And he says, "Aw, I couldn't *stand* you," and I said. "Great, you don't want me, don't worry about it." Jim realized that for once he was not hurting me; it was just "Look, I don't want you," and my reply was just "Good, you don't want me, don't worry, I'm not too worried about you, either, I just live here," and a very striking handsome person suddenly knew, Wait a minute. What I'm saying I feel about her, she actually now feels about *me!* And he was going in the drawer for a gun. The habit of turning and using my hands as a gesture probably saved my life, because when I did I saw him as he came out with the gun, and I got to him and grabbed his arm. Remember, there were two people downstairs, but nobody was going to come up, because they heard me say, "Put down that gun!" And this guy just banged this gun over my head. I had on a summer strapless dress, and in a minute I felt something going drip, drip. And the drip, drip, drip was blood. It was the wildest thing, because I just felt so calm, and I said, "Just a minute, is this what you wanted to see?" I must have leaned against the wall, and the blood was dripping down it. For some reason I was thinking about the fact that I'd just had this house painted. We'd only gotten this house because he had talked me into it. I never realized back then that he used me to break into the neighborhood. I didn't even give it a thought. It was just moving into a new house. He had a helluva brain. A brilliant man, but he was cunning, too.

And this nut stopped, and I said, "Oh, my, the paint." Then I went into the bathroom, got a towel, and he never bothered me anymore. He went back and lay down.

I went downstairs, got in the car, taking my niece with me. I knew exactly what I was going to do, but I could feel myself getting woozy. I drove right over to his parents. I remember going up the steps—it was about seven in the morning—and when I got to the door, I said, "I just came over to let you . . ." and I guess it was probably incoherent, because I don't remember anything more.

They took me up to one of the back rooms and called their family doctor, because if I'd have gone to the hospital, Jim would have been put in jail. When the family physician came up I said, "I don't want to go to sleep. Just patch my head and let me go home." But he gave me a shot and I guess it knocked me out; I didn't wake up till about two in the afternoon. I came downstairs, and there was Jim sitting in the living room, waiting to take his wife home. We went back to our house, and when I got over there I saw he had cooked a duck and he was going to have a great Sunday dinner. He figured we would go out and have a little beer and everything would be great.

I fixed my hair neatly over the patch and left that Monday morning. I was getting ready to open in *Bless You All* at the Mark Hellinger. He said, "Great. I'll be there for the opening Wednesday. See you Wednesday, kiddo." And I left. The show opened and I got a wire: "I'd like to send you some flowers, but I'm broke. Do you have any money?" I thought, "Dear heart, you know it just dawned on me, I'm getting a little older now. If I have to give somebody money to send me flowers, then I don't need a flower."

I didn't go back to Washington that week. The calls would come in just about show time, you know, just before half-hour, and he would say, "What do you think I'm doing? I'm in your house. I'm in your house and me and my ——" and the dirty words, you know. "We're having a ball and we're using your dishes." I said, "Great, have a ball."

One night, Mr. Noel Coward came in to the Blue Angel, and in an offhand way I was talking about the marital situation and this business of calling. I asked, "What do you *do?*" And he sat down at the table—we were sitting out in the lounge and Bobby Short was playing the piano—and I said, "He's calling just about a half hour before the show starts, and how do I work when I've got someone like that antagonizing me? I take these things up with me on the stage."

He said, "Darling, don't let anyone bother you before you go on the stage. Don't let anyone give you anything on your mind to go out there with. If he calls up and starts to antagonize you or say nasty things, just don't even listen to it. Just hang up the phone, go take yourself a roll in the hay, get up, wash, smoke a cigarette, and forget it."

Oh, how the English can express sometimes! I told my stage manager that from that night on, I would accept no calls, particularly any long-distance calls from Washington, D.C., and from then on I had a beautiful attitude about everything.

Now, the guy moved out again. On my day off I came back home and was upstairs in my bedroom. I had two boxer dogs downstairs and a chain on the front door. And I heard this bang, bang, bang, around two at night. Then I heard a rip and these two dogs started snarling. Jim had been driving by and saw the light up in my bedroom. And now this guy thought, "Oh, boy, somebody's with Pearl . . ." He was jealous now, it hit him—he was *out* now. I went to the head of the stairs, and he was coming up the stairs. I said, "What are you doing to my door?" The door was off the hinges, chain and all. So I said, "Oh, you can't do that." I was rather amazed at myself. There was nobody in there but two dogs and myself, and at this point, I didn't want to see nothing—you should excuse the expression—called man. Believe me.

Well, somehow this guy eased himself in, and I said, "Okay, I feel sorry for you, but you have to sleep in *that* room. You're welcome, but you have a bedroom and I have a bedroom, too." Next morning I went down and told the lawyer, "Look, tell him he can't come in."

Maybe the worst of it was the time that Jim tried to have me committed. I knew Jim had been "Gaslighting" me. I had seen the Bergman picture, so I knew what was happening. For instance, I'd have my keys on the table and they'd disappear. I'd say, "Where are the keys?"

"They're not here."

"The keys, I just left them there on the table."

"Oh, you moved them."

I was really beginning to think something was wrong with me. When I went for the sugar, my coffee would maybe disappear. I would ask, "Where is the coffee?"

"You drank it."

"*I* drank it?"

And so on.

I still don't know the *why* of it. Anyway, while in New York, at Jim's suggestion I went for a checkup. The whole thing was getting to me. I heard a man of science say, "Has she got any money?" The doctor wanted me to draw a face. I drew an egg, and put in big eyes. I wouldn't answer questions. Jim said, "She takes benzedrine tablets." We had some, from his uncle's drugstore. *He* got the pills to stay awake driving.

From there I went to Washington for another checkup. The doctor was a friend that Jim had gone to college with.

Looking back, I could have had that doctor's license so fast it wasn't funny. Jim had said "checkup," but I suspected something else now, and I just withdrew. There comes a time when you've got to close out everybody, not looking to see what their purpose is; you can't believe your loved ones would really want to hurt you. You say, "Let me just wilt and die." I was as perfectly sane as I'm sitting here. It's just that if you keep talking to me and I don't want to hear you, I can look at you all day and register nothing. The doctor said, "She's a blank," and I was looking right at him. Then he said, "We'll go in the room here," and I know he's going to put me on the table and take a sample of my blood and check my reflexes.

Well, I was lying on this table, and the doctor put this thing on my arm, and all of a sudden, dear God, I went somewhere. Something seemed to just hit me inside my head, and I thought, "Oh, dear God, what's happening. I'm going in a hole. Something is happening to me." All I knew was that I was falling into a pit. I looked at my arm and he wasn't taking blood out, but I saw something going in there. And it was really hitting me and, dear God, let me hold on.

It must have been minutes that I was just holding on, and nobody could tell me there wasn't something big in all this. Unfortunately, the gentleman took too much time to say, "What's your name?" "How old are you?" and so forth, and I must have begun to come out of it sooner than he expected. The hole got a little shallower, and I thought, "Oh, dear God, they're doing something to me," and I could see him at the foot of the table, the doctor sitting there. That man asked me questions that you wouldn't ask a dog. And I lay there for about an hour; I told him everything. "You see, Jim has that girl . . ." and blah, blah, and I told him everything in the book about that rascal. Now this, remember, is his college friend.

Suddenly I got sick of both of them, and I looked at this man and I said, "You know, doctor, I could baffle scientists."

And this man looked at me and said, "In other words, you have known exactly what I was getting at."

I said, "For the first few minutes I didn't, but you bet your ass I have for the last hour, or however long I've been here, and I want to tell you something before I get up." (I didn't know at that point even what I'd had, but he'd given me truth serum.) I said, "You realize I can get right up off this table and pull your license down off the wall. I am a normal, sane person, walked into your office for a checkup, and you gave me something without asking me."

"Yes, you could." Now he was frightened. He didn't show it, but you could see, you know, he thought, "Well, Jesus, what if she tells somebody."

And I said, "Yes, but I'll tell you what. You went to school with Jim? I'll make you a bet. Whatever your bill is, you'll never get it from him. I'll probably have to end up paying you for giving it to me."

And it was the funniest thing, this man tried to collect his sixty dollars and he didn't get it. Then one time he met me later on. And he said, "I could never forget you, what a hell of a thing you did, because I could have had my career at an end."

Jim had told this man things. Obviously, he was trying to create something where he could commit me. Why, I don't know—but bless him now.

Finally, after two years of marriage it was over. Oh, I got the house all right. As I said, all the mortgages were in my name, anyway! I didn't even know who was involved with it, or who to go to about it. I didn't know anything about mortgages and this, that and the other. It was all tied up with a friend of Jim's who had bought the second trust at 6 per cent and somebody else who bought the third trust. I was about $70,000 in debt. Everything was gone.

One night after the show I was in Beefsteak Charlie's on Fifty-second Street around the corner from the Zanzibar on Fiftieth Street. I was just sitting there when Nina Mae McKenny, the great colored actress, sat down by me. She was in *Hallelujah,* a beautiful and talented woman ("The Girl with the Big Brown Eyes") She told me that a cousin of hers was looking for a house. And I said, "She is?" She said, "Her husband's a dentist, and they've got a couple of kids and their house is too small." I said, "Do you want a house? Great. You got a house. I'll give you the key. It's all furnished. I left everything, sweetheart." I moved the gas stove out (five years later), and left the rest. They paid fifty dollars a week, and anything they wanted, so long. I never bothered if they didn't pay. I just left rugs, the whole thing, brand-new furniture, everything—just left it. Because that was material. Of course, it was dumb as I think of it now.

Jim married the nineteen-year-old girl friend, and she managed to cope with him for just about three or four months.

God has given him rest now, and though there was agony, there were beautiful moments, too—and I often smile and cry at both. It takes a lot of living to get perspective on such painful times, but now I can look back on Jim with understanding and sorrow rather than anger or pain. Rest well, dear heart, and know I understand, as I know all of us involved did before the sleep came.

5

Even when I was suffering setbacks in my personal life, my career continued to grow. New opportunities came along, and I tried new things. My first call to the theatre was *St. Louis Woman* in 1946, music by Harold Arlen, lyrics by Johnny Mercer, book by Arna Bontemps and Countee Cullen, and directed by Rouben Mamoulian. Lena Horne was originally considered for a role as the leading lady, then something went astray and we ended up with Ruby Hill, a very talented new actress. The Nicholas Brothers (who were well known by now from the movies), Rex Ingram, a fine actor, and this vaudevillian, me, were in the cast. Acting sounded exciting to me; but, then, I thought we acted in vaudeville, too, so maybe the difference wouldn't be that great. (Lady, you had a lot to learn.)

We went into rehearsal while I was still at the Zanzibar, but by the time we got deeply involved in the play my engagement there had ended. My part was not so large, but all the songs were just great. The big number, as sometimes happens, did not turn out to be the showstopper, and yet now it's a classic: "Come Rain or Come Shine."

Would you believe that Lucky Duck Me had the two show-stoppers: "A Woman's Prerogative," and "Legalize My Name." For that play I received the Donaldson Award, for my debut as an (excuse me) actress.

Mr. Rouben Mamoulian, one of the good people in my life, and his lovely wife Azadia and I became dear friends during that play. He's truly one of America's best directors, and it was my privilege to work on two plays with him. Later in our lives *(Porgy and Bess)*, something happened (a big controversy over the making of the picture) and during this, many friendships were either broken or mis-understandings arose. We haven't seen each other since to know what really went on, but I will always think of them as the lovely people I met the first day of *St. Louis Woman*, and regardless of other circumstances I love them.

We were rehearsing at the Martin Beck Theatre, getting ready for the Philly opening, and I caught such a cold that they gave me two days off. When I returned, the cast was in an uproar. The mumbling had grown as loud as thunder. It had to do with the funeral scene. In that scene June Hawkins had killed her lover, and when she came to the grave she was to fall on her knees and raise her hands to heaven. That, in turn, was to make everyone else sad enough to do the same. Well, sir, that gesture only served to make the cast angry. They felt it was too Negroid. We kept going over and over that scene, and Mamoulian was displeased with it because he sensed something lacking and didn't know what it was.

Although all of us were unhappy, no one had opened up to tell him they didn't like it. My bony knees got tired of bending. Finally, he asked them why the scene didn't have the feeling and—what do you know?—no one opened his damn mouth. I got so angry at them for all their grumbling and then being afraid (or whatever). I said, "Why don't you tell him what you don't like?" Again no voice was raised. So I told him what the trouble was. He stopped the rehearsal, came onstage, took a chair, and asked us all to sit in ours. Then he proceeded to tell us of his coming to this country, how he got nothing much at first, then came *Porgy*, which became a classic. He reminded everyone of the great contribution the Negro had made to America, giving the country its only original art: music. Then he dismissed us, and out of that came some new feelings and better relationships.

One day, as I came offstage, I saw everyone looking up the stairs at a member of the cast, who was chasing the stage manager up toward a landing. Not a person moved. Then "Fearless Pearl" went bounding up just as landings ran out and the fellow had the stage manager in a corner, holding a fire axe over his head. I screamed, "Stop it, stop it!" and he dropped the axe. Often I see that man I saved; he is still a stage manager but on a big TV show. He walks over, puts his arm around me, and smiles. He may even still see the axe. Who knows? All I can say is that I was not a heroine. But when you love people, sometimes you don't stop to think of your personal danger.

Sometimes the dramatic actors gave me a hard time. (The Nicholas Brothers were also from vaudeville, so we were oddities.) While onstage I could hear them in the wings saying, "An actor wouldn't say a line that way," or "She turns her back to the audience." The audience paid me in love and applause. True, shows are destroyed onstage, but I've seen more destroyed by the attitudes of the people backstage. When you bicker with each other in the back, how can you go out and smile with sincerity onstage?

My second try at legit was in *Arms and the Girl*, with Nanette Fabray, Georges Guetary, and John Conte. The play opened on Broadway to mixed notices, but I came through okay. There was another star in the show, a horse. I mustn't forget him. From the beginning there were misgivings about that horse, because they are show stealers, like children. Then, too, you can't pin down what they might do onstage.

His entrance always brought a gasp from the audience. He was so good-looking (and knew it). But Nanette and I (plus a few others) were beginning to feel time was running out, and soon he would do an act of his own. He had been rearing up for a few nights, as if bored by something, and his restlessness was upsetting to the cast. The actor who rode him was portraying George Washington, and he came to our village at the finale to tell off Nanette, who had been disturbing the entire Revolutionary War.

I guess the horse decided to take matters into his own hands (or whatever horses take matters into) and show these humans how little they knew about animals. The next night we were in place for the finale, waiting for George's great entrance. George came in on his white charger, who looked mighty happy (as I think of it now). He must have been thinking, "Boy, I'm going to lay something on these humans that will make history."

Nanette and I were standing by a house in the village, looking apprehensive, as we had for the last couple of nights, when plop, plop, plop, it fell. I heard Nanette say, "Oops" and, boy, the entire place went to pieces. It took the audience and cast awhile to realize what had happened, but when they did, the band went to pieces, the audience was hysterical, the cast laid out on the stage, doors were being flung open. Mr. Horse, with George aboard, took the biggest dump in history. I must give the actor credit; he sat tall in the saddle.

When the curtain went down, someone had to clean it up. You know unions. Two men were asked to do the job. My dressing room was just offstage, so I could hear the conversation. One man was saying, "Wait until my union hears about this." Then the scraping of the shovel. Those two guys were raising the devil, and all I could do was laugh my fanny off and think, "Well, fellows, in what union would this job go?" The Sanitation Department takes care of it in the street, but for the stage, I don't know. The horse must have told all his friends what he did to us that night. He wasn't fired, and I had a feeling the next night he was smiling again.

St. Subber gave me my first *starring* role on Broadway. I played the madam in *House of Flowers,* Madame Fleur. Harold Arlen wrote as only he can, fantastic! Oliver Messel, that genius, made beauty shine in the scenery and costumes, for which he won awards.

House of Flowers closed much too soon, but that is often the way of our trade. Now, people ask why did it close? There were a million versions. One, untrue, was that Pearl did not cooperate. I like my business and will do all that is asked, and more. However, when these things don't end well, there must be a scapegoat. A number of people could have been blamed. The sadness over that show is a bubble burst for many talented folks, but we've all grown a bit and will meet again.

Peter Brook left the shores of England to direct. He's a very brilliant man. Geoffrey Holder, Carmen De Lavallade, and Diahann Carroll all worked diligently. So where did it go wrong? This you could ask of many Broadway shows which go down the drain, but, rest assured, none worked harder than your girl here. I gave myself to it, one hundred per cent—not ninety, not seventy, but one hundred.

While we were in rehearsal, a lady named Marlene Dietrich used to bring us coffee and pastries. We'd met at the Blue Angel, and I knew the warmth of the woman, but during this period I really saw the person. I'll always remember an amusing incident which happened during an opening night in Philadelphia. During intermission my feet were killing me, per usual. Back came this elegantly dressed Marlene, and she started to help me rub them. They were so everlasting sore that even Dietrich in all her glory couldn't help. It was pretty funny to me to think of this glamour girl of the screen offering to ease my agony. This was a lady I'd always seen on the movie screen, and it was too much to believe. Beneath that legend there beats a heart. There's understanding.

It is rare to find a young performer with that extra spark of real showmanship. I saw it at once in Diahann Carroll when, in her teens, she played in *Carmen Jones* with me. I wanted her in *House of Flowers*, too. As the madam of the house, one of my "flowers" I was to think of like my own daughter. I wanted her to have a handsome and rich husband. I protected her more, and she was supposed to be the only virgin that I had in the place.

Well, I asked for Diahann in this part. She was about eighteen at the time. I told them that I knew her and I could feel the warmth from her, and they picked Diahann for the show. We remained great friends, and Diahann has made very great strides.

Hearing the overture is what I like most about being in legit theatre (it's a warm feeling)—and that curtain bow for a job done. It makes you really feel a part of the theatre, that great sense of belonging. Vaudeville is a marvelous stepping stone to legit and movies. You learn to touch the audience, yet leave them alone, which no other part of the business teaches you so well. Sometimes a performer can become so much a part of the show business world that he loses touch with the people, the audiences, outside. It's good to be, as the Bible says, in the world but not of it.

Well, I had tried vaudeville and the clubs, and then legit. And I didn't stop there, because new offers came in.

One day a long-distance call came from New York City, from Mr. Kalcheim of the William Morris Agency, which now represents me. He asked if I was sitting in a strong chair. I answered yes. He said, "Remain seated—so you won't fall over from shock when I tell you this goodie. You're going to do a movie called *Variety Girl*. It's a three-week deal, and you get twenty-five thousand for it."

Contracts were signed, and Hollywood-bound was I. No coach, no bus, but a bed on the big time "Chief!" Live it up, honey! I had slept on the train USO-style (berth), but this time I had a private room.

After *St. Louis Woman,* a lady in the chorus had told me that there wasn't much work around for the type of singing she did. She asked if I needed a maid to travel with me. Now, this was something that had never entered my mind, though I was taking on many more responsibilities. Zelda was in her forties. I thought she would be like a mother. (Unfortunately, I didn't realize I was getting older, and sometimes she became too much of a mother.) So Zelda went along, and we checked into a hotel in Hollywood.

The first week they didn't even call me to the studio. My manager, Chauncey Olman, and his wife Sybil were with me. I should have mentioned earlier in the book how our relationship started. I was with Nat Nazarro, and it wasn't going well, so one day with five cents' subway fare, I went to the office of a man I'd heard was a brilliant lawyer. This man listened to my story, went to work, and in time got my release, and, believe me, no one was released from Nazarro without a fight. But Chauncey was pretty brilliant himself. I asked him to be my manager, also to lend me the fare to get back uptown. That's dear Chauncey, who recently (in 1965) walked up eight flights during the New York blackout and fell dead. This man came to my rescue at all times, no questions asked.

When I got my first check, it was for eight thousand three hundred and thirty-three dollars. I got a brown paper sack and went around the corner from Paramount Studios to the bank with the check. These people looked at me as if I were a different kind of bank robber. After a great consultation in the back, and two or three executives giving me the eye, they filled my sack and off I went. We spread the money on the floor and walked on it, looked at it, prayed over, and fondled it. Then came the big plans: what to do with it.

Chauncey had seen this kind of money before, but not me. His suggestion was to save some, buy myself a nice stone and some nice clothes. The next day we went to Ruser and McCormick and picked out a two-carat ring (mercy me, it looked like the Hope Diamond), then to Adrian's for suits, and I can't tell you how many goodies I picked up for family and friends. Then I returned to my room, spread them all on the floor, and enjoyed them fully. The banking part came hard. I wanted to spend it all, but I listened and put some shekels away.

The second week I had a dress fitted for my part in the movie and bought shoes. Then came the second check. Back to the bank, paper sack, cash, shopping spree, and "stomping over the change." Why I cashed it, I don't know, unless I wanted to see what that much money looked like. Cinderella never had it so good, even after the Prince fitted the shoe. I still hadn't been asked to really hit a lick on the movie.

Variety Girl was a picture dealing with the wonderful work the Variety Clubs do all over the country for everyone, regardless of race, religion or creed, and everyone on the Paramount lot was in it. This was a chance to see all the big stars, at one time or another, shooting scenes. Came the third week and it was finally time to go to work.

The scene for me was with a lot of women at a club meeting, and I was supposed to walk in (Miss Know-It-All) and tell them in song how to handle their men. My dress, by the fabulous Edith Head, was gold threaded, molded to the figure, shoes with heels so cotton-picking high I felt I was on stilts, with one strap around the ankle. Not only did they hurt, they were too fancy for me. Added to all this were six sable scarves (looked like plain rat to me) and a feather in the hair. Pearlie Mae was delicious-looking, but miserable as all hell, longing for dear old vaudeville, and that lovely loneliness I enjoy on the stage. To top it off there were these women. The way I work, I *imagine* folks in my songs, and suddenly here they were, big as day, and some of them bigger than day or night. Not being used to this acting business, I was scared, and my pet hate was staring at me: the camera.

Now came the lady brushing my hair, wardrobe people pulling at the skirt, prop men handing me something— well, I was fit to be tied. I was doing what I was told, but this new world was frightening me. Having made a flicker or two, I now realize that's how the movie industry is run, but, darling, your première appearance in this world can be a little shaky.

In this scene, I was to enter the room and drape around a post, then the women would gather around while I sang an all-knowing song about men. Dear, dear, I'm the worst draper. Lena Horne and Josephine Baker can do this, but with my feet killing me, I just get across a room, and when I find a post I don't drape, I lean. Frank Loesser had written a crazy song for me, and it would have been great for the scene, but we had an obstacle. Actually, we had four obstacles: two breasts and two eyes, all belonging to one of the women in the background. Wherever I went, the breasts and eyes were there. They photographed from every angle, but there they were, and at that time in the movies they weren't really wrapped up in bosoms. (Had they been, this scene would have been a smash!) Danny Dare, the man who put me in the picture, had seen me at the Zanzibar, I found out later (and I'm grateful he had), so what came off in the rushes obviously was not what he was looking for.

Danny asked me how I felt and I told him like a damn fool. He asked what did I think I could do. I said, "Though 'Tired' has now been out over a year, it's very popular. Give me a rocking chair, feather duster, coffee table, sofa, a huge mirror (ah!), and a throw rug." I wanted to act as if I were in my own home, waving goodbye to my hubby, then go into telling him off. The icing on the cake was to let me wear a plain house dress and some flat comfortable shoes.

He agreed to this, put two cameras on me, yelled for a rehearsal. I kicked off the shoes (they were miserable, too) and went to town. When I finished, they yelled, "Cut and print." Around to the bank, paper sack, and that was it.

Soon I had a call to go into another picture, *Isn't It Romantic?*, with Veronica Lake—and so back to Movieland.

On our arrival this time in California (and after one night in the hotel where we stayed before) we heard about a lady named Rose Tizol, married to a famous musician, who might let me stay with her. She didn't have a regular rooming house, just a few friends she'd rent to. Zelda went around to see the Tizols. Juan is one of the best valve trombone players going. He's also one of the original Ellington men and wrote the music for "Perdido" and (with Duke) for "Caravan," both jazz classics.

Zelda went to check on the room while I was at the studio spending a first and exciting day. She returned and went into a description of the house and my room in such glowing terms that I was almost afraid to go there. I sent her rushing to get the luggage from the hotel before the woman changed her mind.

It turned out that Zelda had also given a mental picture of me to the Tizols that matched every inch of the house and more. They were as ready for me as I was for their house. When I got over there, Juan opened the door and I could see a lady, Rose, descending this wide staircase very grandly. She greeted me formally, too. (Later, I found out that neither of them could care less for any of the fancy stuff.) She was evidently waiting for the star to shine, but no glow came. Rose showed me to my room, and it was even more than Zelda had said, just gorgeous. The bath was larger than the room I'd just moved from, but I didn't tell Rose that until later.

After she left, I drank in the beauty of my new home, rolled around on the rugs. (You didn't know that, did you, Rosie?) True, I came from a nice clean home, but this was furnished like nothing I'd ever seen. Remember, Juan had been in our business for some time and, not being people who drink or smoke, they put their money into their love: their home.

Hunger struck me at last, but I had no idea where to go to get a good meal. I trudged down the stairs and asked Rose. She said nothing nice was close, but told me of a number of places I could drive to. Then she offered the *pièce de résistance*. She said, "You can eat with us if you like and look around tomorrow." Her fare, she said, was simple.

But it wasn't. She cooked like mad. I asked her if I could eat with her all the time. Well, she said, in that case she would have to lay in some steaks and chops, and I wanted to know why. I finally said, "Juan, please tell your wife I'm a plain person, and neck bones and beans suit me just fine."

Rosie said, "Honey, do you eat that kind of food?" and I knew then and there I'd been described as a star to her, but obviously a heavenly one. We often laugh about our stupid first meeting, how stiff it was and silly. Mrs. Brown (her mother), at that time seventy-seven years young, and William, seventeen, were the rest of my new family. Mrs. Brown and I would chitchat and cream our faces like two schoolgirls.

Paramount became a home for me. Besides these first two movies, I also made *That Certain Feeling* and *St. Louis Blues* (with Nat Cole) there. A word about *St. Louis Blues*. I played Nat's auntie, and we often laughed about that. I was working at the Flamingo Hotel in Vegas for Mr. Parvin, and for three weeks I commuted. I'd do the show, leave in a car at 1:30 A.M., arrive at the studio in time to dress at 8 A.M., finish at 3 P.M., catch a plane (which most of the time was late), arrive in Vegas to bathe and get ready for two shows at eight-thirty and midnight. This went on for the entire picture. (The worst thing I do to myself is overdrive.) My other films, *Fine Young Cannibals, Porgy and Bess,* and *Carmen Jones,* were at other studios. With such a small number of films under my belt, I never had a chance to "go Hollywood."

Although I got my start in movies at Paramount, one of the most interesting of my Hollywood experiences came a few years later, when Mr. Samuel Goldwyn decided to film the classic *Porgy and Bess.* It was a big project. Naturally, with an all-colored cast, we expected the usual controversy to start before the filming got off the ground, and it did. Talk began: What treatment would the story get? A million problems were brought up, but Goldwyn forged straight ahead. Sidney Poitier, that fine actor, was Porgy. Sammy Davis was Sportin' Life, Dorothy Dandridge was Bess, and Brock Peters played Crown, the villain. Ruth Attaway played Serena, and yours truly was Maria.

The cast was assembled, fittings went on, and soon the call for work came. We were to report at 7 A.M. to the stage, in costume, so that the production people could see how the show would look all together. Big as some of the dresses and petticoats were, it's a wonder we could all get on the same stage. I know it was in a slum area that the characters lived, but I have yet to figure out why no one in the cast was supplied with shoes. If the characters ever worked for someone in the town, they would have been given some hand-me-downs. I positively told Costuming and anyone concerned that I would not risk catching pneumonia running around with no shoes on, so I was granted a pair of slides to wear. Others got shoes, too. The poorest section of any town is not doing that bad! Neither did I cover my head with a bandanna scarf. There is no place in the world where females dress identically—they don't like each other that much.

There were some in the cast who wanted to go along

with the dialect bit, because, they said, "Honey, that's the flavor." Well, it tasted like mud in 1958. I said I would have to go to a "language school" to learn how to get out some of the "dese" and "dose." The script called for an exaggerated accent, but the director didn't want it. I mentioned it at the reading-through of the script. We had been told to take out anything offensive to us, but some kept reading that old version. One fellow and I had a clash of words in rehearsal about it.

The day we were to report, I set my clock for 5 A.M., but there was a call to the hotel. We were not to come near the studio. It was in flames and all traffic was being diverted from the area.

I had never met Goldwyn until we were called into his office to hear the details of what was to happen. Here was and is a "giant"—a very impressive-looking man, not handsome but wise. Everyone was there, including Mrs. Goldwyn and all the department heads. All the seats were taken, and some sat on the floor. There was a hassock left at the front of Mr. Goldwyn's desk, and I took it. This man started to tell us of his beginning in the movies. He talked on for a long time. I imagine there was a tiny smile on my face, and he saw it. He looked at me and asked, "What are you smiling at, young lady?" I said, "Well, I was just sitting here thinking how good God has been." My meaning was that we were supposed to have been at the studio at 7 A.M. Heavens! If that fire had started two hours later, there wouldn't have been one person left alive. It would have been one of the greatest disasters ever. That was nearly the largest sound stage in Hollywood.

With nothing to do for eight weeks until they rebuilt things, we—meaning me and my husband, Louis Bellson, whom I married in 1952 (and I'll tell you all about that later)—went to Chicago to fill in the time. Louis wanted to do band work there.

While we were in Chicago, one Sunday morning Louis complained of a small pain, and said he'd walk around to the hospital. This guy never opens his mouth to complain about anything, so it frightened me a little. After an hour I got more worried, so I walked over to the hospital. There was Louis, still sitting in the waiting room patiently. The doctor said it might be an upset stomach and gave him some aspirin or something. All day he was in agony, and that night insisted on going to work. The first show over, he came into the dressing room to lie down (which was rare), and soon I called a doctor. He told Louis not to do the last show, but in vain. Finally the doctor said, "When the show is over, you go to the hospital for a checkup. It may be your appendix." The show was great, but I was watching a man suffering and sweating like mad. (Lou plays two bass drums.) Then he was whisked away, and my friend Lois and I sat all night waiting for the results of the checkup. Around 9 A.M. I couldn't stand it any longer; I called and asked about Mr. Bellson. The lady on the phone said, "The appendectomy went fine." Not understanding her, I repeated myself, and she said it again. Stupefied, I asked, "Will he be working tonight?" She said, "Usually they don't work right after an operation."

Yipe! It hit me! What operation? Lord, this woman has said *appendix!* You should have seen the outfit I put on to get to this hospital at least six miles away. Orange jump suit, beige straw hat, sandals, black purse. I didn't know what the hell I was putting on. There was one thing in my mind—my husband.

On arrival, I hollered as I went through the door, "Who cut my husband?" probably scaring everyone in the waiting room. I livened the place up quite a bit. Here I was right in the town and nobody had even called to say they were operating on Louis! What if something had happened and I'd been home thinking it was a "checkup"? After much talking, they took me up to see him. I got as far as the door, took a look, and the next thing I knew the nurse was waving ammonia over me. Lou appeared so helpless lying there! I'd never seen him ill.

Every day I went to see him, and he was a happy man spreading love to all who entered the room. But that's the man.

About that time the news came that Mr. Mamoulian was *not* going to direct the picture. It was a real shock because Mamoulian had done the original *Porgy.* Otto

Preminger took over, and the people who were fussing over the whole project from the beginning began to fuss some more. Organizations were saying that Preminger would not understand the Negro. This hurt me; frankly it took the joy out of working with an old and dear friend again. He is a fine director, and when I'd worked with Preminger before, I had not experienced any such things as these organizations were talking about. It wasn't fair. My thinking might have been different if these statements about racial matters hadn't gotten ugly. If he feels anything of that sort, he hides it well. Oh, he hollers! I think that helps his day. He's a perfectionist. But, anyway, Mamoulian had to step aside, and I know it must have been a heartbreaking thing for him to see his "baby" done by someone else.

Dorothy Dandridge, "Bess," was very dear to me. Dottie was so immaculate, what I call a real "Miss Priss." Having worked with her on *Carmen Jones* and *Porgy and Bess*, I'd seen the real Dorothy come through a few times— the soul of a warm, wonderful girl. Dottie became a pet project of my heart. And that was my other name for her, "Pet Project." I always wanted to see her in a peasant-necked dress, soft. This was truly a girl of simple tastes, who was put on that pedestal our business is famous for. Instead of telling her some of the things that were not quite right, telling her when she was famous and strong enough to get knocked down, some waited—until it was too late.

I used to put her on, making her laugh at her own actions sometimes. Once she was angry because I was telling her some facts of life, and she said, "Pearlie Mae, I don't know what makes you tick, tick, tick." My answer was simple and direct. "I am a ——— [not such a nice word] clock!"

In 1964 she used to telephone me at intervals for some months. I couldn't figure out why, because I didn't think we'd ever become real close—at least not to the point of going to parties or visiting each other's home. (Once, though, I remember, she did come to a party at our ranch, one of the three parties we had in nine years.) And sometimes she would avoid me in a strange way.

The last time we met she cried in her confused mind. The pity of it, she was so tired inside. No one wanted her, she felt. Visions of great pictures she was to make. We were having a wardrobe fitting as nurses for a screen test. The next day we had the test, and Dorothy, bless her heart, was still confused. She held my face in her hands and she said, "If I don't get the part, I hope you do." That was in June 1965.

On September 8, 1965, Louis and I were at Lake Tahoe (where Louis was working with Duke Ellington). I'd gone to the market for groceries for dinner and I was "putting on the pots." I'll never be out of work, no sir, because Mama taught me to cook. Then Louis was on the phone; he looked up sadly and said, "Dorothy is dead." He was talking to our housekeeper in California, Mrs. Longton, and she told him that a few days before her death Miss Dandridge had been calling to say that she was back from Mexico. We found out later that she'd broken a little bone in her foot and somehow a piece had gotten into her bloodstream, and that was it. But at that point all I knew was that she was suddenly dead.

I sat down at the table, got pencil and paper, and poured out my feelings for Dottie. I knew it was too late to talk to her, but it helped me:

> Today Dorothy Dandridge's life ended. I wonder how many of those who fawned over this beautiful child of God will mourn her. Couldn't anyone see the confusion? So long ago it happened. And everyone sat back and ignored a piece of lost humanity living in a world of falsehood, trying to find someone to understand. None came near. They were not afraid of what they saw; they only waited it out. Anyone would have been able to see that the Dorothy on top was concealing the true beauty.
>
> Dottie, though we met seldom, I am going to miss you here on this earth. Rest well, sweet child, the pain is over. Only those who are left, those who have

things they should have said or done, will suffer. Somehow I wish we could have talked. Strange, you called me only a week ago and said you were going to Mexico and didn't want to leave without saying goodbye. I hear you always, dear friend. Only one question will always remain: Could I have helped you? As Louis said to me, you know I surely would have tried.

Pet Project, so long.

6

———◆———

These days there are basically three kinds of performers, in terms of their popularity. There are the cold ones, the medium ones, and the hot ones. The cold ones you can't give away. Lots of them were hot ones last season. The medium ones have had some success, but are still looking for that big peak. The hot ones are often red burning hot, but they tend to fade. Then, in addition, there are some performers who are not in any of these groups—they are the legends: Waters, Crosby, Chevalier, Durante, Sinatra.

What is really sad is when a legend starts to fade. I think about the cowboys who carved notches in their guns for every man they killed. Everything the person has done is right there. You can see the experience in them. But sometimes, though the gun still has bullets and the aim is still good, the world stops the carving of the notches. It is so sad to see a legendary performer cut off from his audiences, even though the basic talent is still there, seasoned by experience. Who throws away a beautiful old bottle of wine?

I've had the chance to meet quite a few of the legendary personalities through the years, and I never seem to get over the excitement of it.

In 1941, during the war, we played at a base in a place called Las Vegas. When you got off the train there was the main street, and inside all of these places people were throwing dice and playing slot machines, with policemen looking on. None of us had seen anything like it before, and, at that time, other than people who'd been abroad to Monte Carlo, other folks in America hadn't seen it, either. We went into these spots and played the machines. (How ironic that a few years later "people of race" were barred, though now they're allowed in again.)

I was booked into the Flamingo Hotel, and at that time only Lena Horne and Arthur Lee Simpkins of the brown race had worked there. There were only two other places then: El Rancho and The Last Frontier. This town was so elegant you couldn't imagine, and nothing like it existed in our country. Vegas yet has to be matched for glitter.

I always set up my dressing room the night before I open, even if I have to wait until three or four in the morning to do it. It makes it not seem too new to me the next day. (And for the last six years, I've rehearsed with the band the day before, for the same reason.) So, as usual, I put a tablecloth on the dressing table to make it a bit nicer.

Having set everything just right, I came in the next night ready for action. And wow! It looked like a magician had been in and done a magic trick: makeup and everything were topsy-turvy. I sent for the backstage manager and asked the reason for it. He said, "We had to take the tablecloth, as Mr. Siegel wants everything accounted for." I asked for another, got it, and, bless my soul, the next night the same thing happened. They removed it again. Holy mackerel! Was this to go on for three weeks? I sent again for the backstage man, and once again he gave me the bit about Mr. Siegel. So I asked him if I could talk to Mr. S. When I came off after the show, a young, dapper, and handsome man was standing by the dressing-room door. Not expecting any visitor, I nodded and started into the room. But he spoke to me. "Did you want to see me? I'm Mr. Siegel."

"Ah! Yes, you can help me, sir." I went into a big explanation of what I wanted: a simple tablecloth. Being a user of my hands, I was by now tapping him on the shoulder and pointing a bony finger in his stomach, getting my point across. Whatever struck me, I'll never know, but I remembered having read this man's name (I am a thorough newspaper reader, want ads and all). "Are you *Bugsy* Siegel?" Suddenly I knew it—this was one of the biggest men in the underworld.

He replied, "My friends call me 'Benjamin,' my enemies 'Bugsy.' "

Now, you know I had no intention of being this boy's enemy. I thought it better to be friendly! He never moved but asked me, "Is there anything else you'd like?"

Well, for some reason, it flashed through my mind how every night, going home, I'd pass a car lot, and at that time the Roadmaster Buick was the thing. I couldn't even drive a bicycle, but I wanted that car, so I told him about one I'd seen. Even if that hadn't been my desire, I was so nervous I could only figure, "Keep talking, Pearl, keep talking about anything."

The tablecloths were piled high as my head the next show, and the following morning on the west side, in front of Mrs. Harrison's house, where I lived, sat that pretty red car. Seems as though he knew these men at the lot, called them, and said that I'd give the down payment before I finished the engagement.

When I was fourteen, my stepfather showed me the art of shifting gears on a car, and I had never forgotten. I jumped into my red car, and off I went down the dirt road and around the block, backing up. It took me a day to get a learner's permit. Then I went back two days later for the real McCoy. The man took me around the block and asked me how long I'd been driving. I told him three days, and he said, "You drive like a champion," and gave me my license. I've been driving like a maniac ever since.

Once my sister Virgie came to Vegas and said she would buy a car if she could drive. By now, I'd graduated to a

Cadillac, so I put her in it, took her to the backwoods where I had learned, showed her the fundamental things, turned on the radio, and got out. Like a nut, I sat on the side of the road in the dirt and let her drive toward me. She backed into a tree (ripped a couple of things off) but, all in all, she gained courage, learned to drive. She went home, bought a car, and is a speed demon now. This again demonstrates that when one loses fear, he's home free.

Well, of course I'll never forget my brush with Bugsy (or rather, Benjamin) Siegel. But there are all kinds of legendary people, and I would like to turn to some who have a little different kind of legend: that marvelous human being, Joe Louis, on the bill with me onstage at the Flamingo, and Sonny Liston, who was training at the Thunderbird Hotel. They let people come in to watch Sonny go through the action. The room was jammed, and all the celebrities were introduced; yet no one got the applause "The Man" did. Joe is a figure alone. He not only was and is a Champion, he's also a good person. I asked him to go into the club with me and Joe broke up. "Doing what?" he asked. I said, "Oh, we'll think of something." He accepted, and Joseph and I started to rehearse about four days before opening. Every time we stopped for a break this big hunk of flesh would add about four pieces of cantaloupe to his stomach—and I'm trying hard to figure out how fruit gives so much strength. Each night I'd say he ate about ten halves of cantaloupe, with a few odds and ends thrown in. We worked up a softshoe together, and a slow song. It was fun, and some nights I'd fence with this rascal. One night (oh! Pearl, you fool, you), I hit him hard in the stomach. Instinct made him protect himself, I imagine, and the next thing I knew I was sailing across the stage, earring knocked off (and my ears are pierced, so it was fastened in). Luckily he used his open palm. Joe says I have the hardest hands of any woman he's seen. Where the strength comes from, I don't know.

After the shows, Joe would come in the dressing room and eat more fruit. Once I saw this man angry, and I don't think anyone else has. I also saw him cry. Don't ask me when, Joe, because I'd never tell you. All I can say is that it was when some human said something unkind, and this big lug was so hurt. Joe Louis is a tribute to his profession, a real asset, not to any particular race or creed, but to the world. To know this man is to learn. And I remind you he is a wise man. Though he says very little, when he does speak it's worthwhile to listen. He has God in him and that is goodness. If there's a person who is a person—"a mensch"—it's Joseph Louis.

Another man I admire is Sammy Davis, Jr., though he's different from Joe. There was quite an honor bestowed on Sammy by the Friars Club. The tribute was held in Beverly Hills at the Hilton Hotel, and Sam asked me to sit on the dais. Up to that time Sophie Tucker was the only woman who had been asked to do that. What a night that was. If memory serves me, there was Sinatra, Humphrey Bogart, Jeff Chandler, Tony Martin, Eddie Cantor, Jack Benny, Gary Cooper, George Burns, and many others. It was frightening sitting up there with the "Tops." Eddie Cantor said to Sammy that it was a tremendous honor, especially when you stopped to think that Bert Williams (whom I think Cantor worked with in Ziegfeld Follies), one of the greatest, never got such a night. I suppose at that time it just wasn't being done. Cantor thought it was sad that this man missed a reception like this.

The audience was the cream of all the entertainment world: TV, radio, movies, and vaudeville. When I arrived at the hotel they took me into a special room, and there were all these men. I was the only female present. I noticed one would talk to another, break up laughing, walk over to still another, talk, same process. Then he would retreat to a spot and mark something on a piece of paper. Soon we were called and marched in to the dais. I sat next to Gary Cooper, whom I admired so much.

The program started, and I realized they were all saying funny things. They were putting Sam on, and each one was outdoing the other. I also noticed that as each one spoke, the rest watched their papers and made marks. Little did I know that they were marking off the joke if the other guy said it first. Scared to death, no paper, and up there with the Champions, I began to feel almost ill. Gary Cooper knocked me out. He was nervous, too, and he said, "At least you can sing. All I can do is grunt." As powerful as the group was onstage, there was more power out front. Then came my time to stand. The knees were weak. All I could think to say for an opening line was, "I have no jokes. I just wore 'stones.'" They cracked up.

If it's frightening to entertain the famous ones in our business, I guess it's just as bad in a different way when your audience is famous in other fields. While I was out digging one day in our garden in California, Louis drove up and handed me a telegram. Mail and telephones are my nemesis, so when Louis handed me this wire, unconsciously I put it in my shirt pocket without opening it. Two days later, still working on my project outdoors, I got another wire. I had on the same shirt, so when I started to put this one in my pocket, I came across the first one. It was from George Murphy, the actor and now Senator. He said, "Pearlie Mae, how do we get to you? We'll have to send the Indians over the Ute Mountains to find you. We want you to entertain at the Press Club affair for the President of the United States." There were no holes dug in my size or I'd have fallen in. The first wire had been from George, too. What a nice man. After great preparation, Mama Pearl was off to the affair.

Bob Hope was doing his usual wonderful job. He spends many hours of his life at these things, and has a ball. Vic Damone and lovely Jane Powell were also on the show. We were only supposed to do a short show, because the President had to leave early.

We were taken to a little room off the main dining room at the Sheraton Park Hotel to wait for Eisenhower. Soon we heard the siren sound of his escort, and in came Ike with that famous smile. Secret Service men were all over. Honey, all I'd seen in pictures was there. One thing I noticed about him was that though he met everyone in the room, he had memorized the name of each person he addressed. He turned and said something to me, and I said, "My mother is a staunch Democrat, and she's going to

have a fit that I met the big Republican, but here I am."
He turned on that smile.

My reception from the crowd was terrific, and though
the thing was pinned down to everyone doing just so much
and positively no more, they yelled for "Bill Bailey." Bob
told me to go back on and I did. The President was quite
a distance from the stage, and when I got ready to leave
the stage, instead of taking a bow I waved at him, and
I could see him wave back. The same night, the President
had his first illness. Everyone was saying, "Pearl, the President was tapping his feet while you were singing." Surely
everyone wasn't ringside, but if it made them happy to
say it, I was also happy hearing he enjoyed it. Later he
wrote a nice letter of which I'm proud.

Next inauguration I was one of the performers to be
called in for the three days. Mama joined me for a day.
Tickets were given to the entertainers for all the affairs
held all over town. Front seats for the parade, a meeting
with the Governors, and the Vice President. At the Ar-
mory, we had a good band and lots of fun with the show.
Then came the calls for "Bill Bailey." I called the bass
player onstage and ad-libbed a bit with him, and it was
even better than usual.

Meeting Richard Nixon later at one of the many big
affairs was a thrill. He asked, "Was that bit with the bass
player ad-lib?" (No one seems to know when I'm kidding
around.)

While I was standing awestruck in the middle of the
room, a man walked up (looked like an old Senator who
had been in Congress for years). He spoke to me: "Young
lady, what are you thinking about?"

I said, "I always thought of riches in terms of money,
and now I'm thinking I'm so rich inside I couldn't spend it."

The "swearing-in" ceremonies were impressive. And I
had a great seat. Some man was showing me to a seat on
the lower level, and the next thing I knew another man
stopped us and said, "This is all wrong." He put me on
the upper level just fifteen rows back of Eisenhower. Supreme Court Justices, Senators, Representatives filed in,
and the ceremonies started. Jeanette MacDonald and Gene

Raymond were there from the movies, and marvelous Marian Anderson sang "The Star-Spangled Banner." All this mass of humanity, about a hundred thousand strong, watching history.

Thinking back, I know I have always been really fascinated with famous people. I recall once way back there, before I had met many of these people, how thrilled I was to find myself rubbing elbows with a famous soubrette.

I got a job in Erie, Pennsylvania. I had never been to Erie, Pennsylvania—that was really traveling now. I was about twenty-two. I was going to get eighteen dollars and my room.

This town was loaded with all sporting people, and the pimps. Ernie Pope had the after-hours spot, at the Pope Hotel. He was a man in his thirties. The mother and father were elderly people. They ran this nice hotel and had the cabaret in the back. I was getting a little older, see, so I could see what was going on, you know, and a couple of the characters there liked me, but still I didn't drink. The jukeboxes were just coming out good, and all I wanted to do was just hear the pretty songs. I was flirting now with everybody, but I didn't know what's going on.

Well, this lady came to see me—her name was Susé Brown—and she had been very prominent. She knew my brother and everything. She was what they called a "soubrette," the one who would do all the singing before the chorus girls came out, and she was really cute, with great big eyes. She'd made a pile of money in the business and now she was loaded and was living in Buffalo, New York. My brother had taken me to see her, so I knew who she was, and I felt excited and important that she came to see me. One of the first fur coats I'd seen ever was hers, the fox stoles and the whole thing. Anyway, she came over one night with some sporting people and I was singing "Don't Worry About Me"—it was very popular then, and I got a lot of tips. She said, "I'm going to get you a job in a wonderful place called Buffalo, New York." Oh boy, I'd never been to a spot like that, and she said, "I'm going to call you up." She just liked me, you know, and she knew

Bill. Well, she did call me up, and I went and got twenty-five dollars.

So Susé helped my career along. I have sometimes had chances to help performers, too. I remember one in particular in 1950. Doubling from "legit" to nightclub is hard, but an offer came for me to do so at the Greenwich Village Inn: a twelve and a two o'clock show. I went down to talk the situation over. The show was just starting, so Chauncey and the bosses went upstairs and I stayed to watch. I made the fourth customer. The chorus girls pranced around. Then a singer came on. His opening tune was "I Can't Give You Anything But Love," and he sang like that four-hundred seater was jammed. He did about four or five numbers. This boy could have been in that room alone and he would have sung the same way. He just wanted to belong in the business. Chauncey came back and we set up an opening show: Marion Bruce (a gorgeous girl and good singer), Maurice Rocco (an exciting personality who stood and played the piano), the Three Rockets (a good dance team), and myself. Then I pointed to the boy singer on the stage, Joe Bari.

The boss said, "We don't need him."

I said, "No him, no show for me." I won. (Really, *they* did, because the boy became famous.)

Three nights after opening, the joint was jumping. People were standing in the streets, waiting to get in. One reason was that all the celebrities were coming down to have a ball in the finale. They'd get up and do what they liked. It was old-time show business again. Bob Hope was in town at the Paramount, Frank Sinatra, Ava Gardner, the Mamoulians, Mr. and Mrs. George Sidney, Ray Evans and Jay Livingston ("Mona Lisa" writers) came by, and all dear friends. Oh, it was crazier than anything New York had seen for years.

There's always a dark cloud to mar the beauty of things and, sure enough, one night I went in, and there was a call from Joe. The bosses had said he would be fired. They liked me, so we had a long talk and they agreed to keep him on, but, to be on the safe side, I told Joe that Bob Hope was letting performers get on the stage at the Paramount. So, since Bob had seen Joe at the club, why not go down? Bob is such a doll he wouldn't turn him down. Joe went, and good thing, because they did let him go at the club, but just in time to leave town with Bob Hope for a thirty-day tour. That boy was Tony Bennett. Tony has proved to be all I saw in the back of that room, and I'm proud to have been a small part of his life.

Two years later, I was playing the Paramount Theatre, and a man knocked on my dressing-room door, saying he was Tony's manager. He handed me a package and told me Tony said it had taken time but he wanted me to know he hadn't forgotten. It was a travel clock, and, Tony, we've been traveling ever since. All this is not told for glory, only to show that God works through others and that's beautiful, and it might enrich many souls.

When I was ill in 1965, Tony called to ask what could he do. Nothing, darling, just let me have your wonderful warmth—always. Antonio, keep going upward and onward, always keeping in mind one of your first songs to your public—"I Can't Give You Anything But Love."

Our lives move faster than lightning. Things are new and changing all the time. By 1951, I'd been in Europe twice. During my trip in 1948, I met the grand lady, Miss Sophie Tucker. Duke Ellington (minus band), the Nicholas Brothers, Kay (Duke's singer), and I played the Palladium in London. I lived just around the corner from Bond Street, where the gentlemen walked past all day wearing their bowler hats. Now it's filled with miniskirts. After our show I went around to the "Prince of Wales" to see the Berry Brothers, whom I knew quite well by now. They were on the bill with the last of the red-hot mamas, Miss Tucker.

Wanting to meet her badly, I asked permission to go to her room, and the doorman assured me she would be most gracious, just knock. I did, and a very nice lady said, "Miss Tucker, there's a young lady here who'd like to meet you," and this booming voice came back, "Come right in, honey. I've got to go to the bathroom and [yes, she said it]." I thought this was a real person, not pretentious. We had a long chat, and every time we met after that we shared a warm greeting.

When I was working in Vegas once, she sent for me to come to her table after the show. I had to smile, for the town was so funny about the racial situation and who was allowed in the main room. (Oh, how they have changed!) It was such a laugh, because you could go in some of the lounges but not the main room. What was the difference? What if you came to town and wanted to catch an act? Though you had worked the club, you were not welcomed as a guest in the main room. Now, of course, that stupidity is over.

Many people believe that celebrities don't experience pain. They say, "You celebrities don't know what the common man goes through, because you go everyplace and you're accepted." Sure, today we get a ringside table and all the trimmings, and when the show goes on, your name is right on the list to be called on or introduced. (If the audience gives you a big hand, you get up and do a number.) But we are not really accepted, only *used*. Half the time the owner is getting a free audition. It doesn't hurt business to have the folks see that your place is where the celebrities hang out. For telling you this, I may lose a few ringside seats, but being farsighted, I see better from the back, anyhow.

Anyway, back when Lady Tucker sent for me, it called for a little thought on the management's part. You didn't say no to Tucker, and folks in show business don't buy that racial jazz. But you had a policy. This time luck played into their hands. In Vegas the rooms clear out immediately after the show, and three men (not one, mind you, but three) came to escort me to the table. I worked there, so how come I wouldn't know how to find a table in an empty café? Anyway, we had a long talk, and Miss Tucker gave me her long green chiffon hankie (she always used one onstage). By now I had some jewelry, so I asked her if I had on too much for the stage.

She said, "No, honey, if you got it, wear it."

I said, "What if folks say I'm getting too fancy? 'I knew you when . . .'"

She replied with a hearty laugh. "Tell them it ain't what *was;* it's what *is*."

The sad thing is that there are so many whose talents have lasted but whose faith has dwindled, through the way they're exploited by others. These others cannot take away our talents, but the business has changed and if an artist doesn't have a place to expose his talents, he's dead. Comes that lack of faith. Many times I feel it creeping up on me and I turn on my Faith Light so strong it goes away.

There are two kinds of talent: man-made and God-given. The God-given no man can take away.

Miss Tucker said, "If you can hold the fort and last long enough, they're going to need you. It ain't how good you are, it's how long you can last. Start doing your best from the beginning, and get some enjoyment out of it."

7

I know if I made fifty thousand dollars a week and no one applauded, I couldn't spend it with joy. I'd throw it away foolishly, for the true payoff is straight from the public. A lot of respect has gone out of show business. Performers used to take really great pride in knowing the greats who had been around a long time. They admired them for their years spent in the business. Now they brush them aside. This is where Europe has the edge on us, for the older their artist, the more respect he gets over there.

Years ago it was a thrill to be a part of what these artists did. If Louis Armstrong was the star, never mind how much applause you got. He was Louis Armstrong, closing the show. Today, one hit record and you've got a star on your hands. Such airs! I say it takes ten years to learn to walk on the stage. After making this monstrous "hit," some of these people are booked into a place for lots of money, and they are so *lost*. Then nothing else happens for them, so what do they do? They go back into their shells, or drink, or use anything to keep themselves believing they are important. They're not to blame for this. It's the ones who exploit these innocent children.

I think we've reached a point in the theatre where the public is being denied what it wants. It's being denied this by quite a few methods. An owner may ask for an act his customers will like, but the act never hears about that because some booker has another performer he wants to put in. They'll say, "Well, you're not in demand," and yet you might walk down the street and find everyone saying, "Hi, when are you coming to our town?" And you begin to wonder, "When *am* I going to their town?" Then you've got people who convince you that nobody knows you. It's the most fantastic thing in the world.

Generally, I like to meet the managers of the clubs myself. Sometimes there is so much distortion with the in-between people that you don't really know where you stand. This makes for some interesting meetings, because though most of the club people think they know how to please a performer, they're never quite ready for me.

I got off the train in Cleveland in April of 1966, and there were three men standing on the platform. The station is kind of down in the ground there, you know. When I stepped off it was late at night. They said, "Welcome to Akron," or something like that. I didn't know them, but I said, "I don't want to go to Akron," or something like that. The room porter was standing there waiting for me to get off, and I knew he said Cleveland, but I started back up the steps because I didn't know them, and it was a dark station. And the man could see that I actually was going to get back on. And he said, "No, I'm just kidding, it's Cleveland." And he introduced himself. He was the owner of the club. I had just seen three men and made up my mind, "Now, wait a minute, I don't feel like no games," so I said, "Why did you come?" because I never like people to meet me. One of the many changes in our business is that nowadays a lot of people—some of the new ones especially—have to be caressed to make them work. They have to have their roses every night. None of this has ever meant a darn thing to me. I always said, "I get the job, you tell me what you want, I do the job." All the caressing, smoothing, doesn't mean a thing. You know, when a man says he wants me to do a benefit, I never want him to send me a car. I have a feeling that he doesn't trust me and just wants to make sure that I'm coming. Now, it could be a courtesy, but nine times out of ten it is not a courtesy that he sends the car.

I said, "Why, no one meets me. I don't like anyone to meet me, and I don't want flowers or fruit or anything. I'd rather just get a cab." But I'm still fencing a little bit, too, because I don't know them. So the man after a while said, "Okay," and they got the luggage and they stopped kidding, you know, and I got in the car with them and off we went. I was to stay at the place where the club was. All the way the two men in the front, which was the owner and another man, were laughing at the third and smallest of the men. I said, "Why are you laughing?" One of them said, "You wait until you get to the motel and we'll explain it to you." Remember, I had gotten off saying I didn't want flowers, I didn't want anyone to meet me. None of this is necessary on the job.

When I got up to the motel room, there was a big card table with about three dozen American Beauties on it. There was a five-pound box of candy. There was every drink that could be known to man: four bottles, everything right stamped on it, and everything—beer, champagne, they'd gone right through the wine and whiskey list. It was supposed to be a wonderful greeting. These men were laughing because the other man had said to them— and in all sincerity, because he was a man who had been in the cabaret business longer—he had said, "Leave it to me. I know exactly what performers like." I didn't know him. But that's what so many performers have come to in this new phase of show business. They have to be so catered to that I guess he thought this was needed. And there it sat. I didn't want any of it. So the saxophone player ate up the five-pound box of candy while he lifted weights. That was a big help for him for the ten days. And the greatest thing I got out of it was that every now and then I said I'd like some coffee and they'd get it for me. I had a beautiful ten days there and they just couldn't believe it. Because it has become a cater-to business.

Well, that's the new ones. Thank God, there's still a few left in the business who are strictly art. But we also have quite a few nightclub managers in the business who are strictly business, and you have to keep your eyes open. For instance, some of these standard performers, who have a steady clientele, get pulled in for Lent or the days right after Christmas, and these are the worst days of the year for the club business. The owners know that these certain performers will insure a certain amount of business no matter when they play.

There's a danger in this for the performer. Maybe he will want to come back to this club during a good time of year. Well, now the management has a weapon. They can say, "Well, we'll just pay you this much, because last time you were here we just did average business." Of course, they don't say that was during the holidays after Christmas. As a matter of fact, some of them will want to talk about the number of people you brought in last time, which does not make sense, either. There are some performers who will jam a place with beer business, and other performers who will bring in two hundred people instead of a thousand, but the two hundred will spend more money in an evening than a houseful. You can't pay salaries on beer, not the salaries nowadays.

Most of the places leave a little booking open so they can grab the real hot ones of the moment, and then they always want to keep that basic performer for the slow periods. And it's funny sometimes what they will use on you when they're talking salary. In 1965 I came back after an illness. I had lost lots of weight and felt good, but I hadn't been working for a while. Three or four of the people in the office greeted me and Louis, my husband. They had hugged and kissed me, then suddenly I don't think they realized that Louis and I were still in the room. They were saying, "Oh, doesn't she look slim and gorgeous," and things like that. They thought I was really in top form. But before, they had asked me to play again but said the salary would be lower because they were a little worried over the publicity that I'd had a heart attack. They were asking me to lower my price by thousands of dollars. So I reached out and touched the one who was saying how gorgeous I looked, and said, "Listen, sweetheart, I've always looked like this." I was just putting him on. I said, "I was always gorgeous."

"No, no, no," he said. "Look at you. You must be thirty or forty pounds lighter."

I said, "And the talent, too?"

He said, "Oh! no, the talent's still heavy as ever."

And I said, "Well, then, tell me something. I thought you people were supposed to be so intelligent. You're offering me a reduced salary for a corpse, and in case I don't make it through the engagement you'll still make a profit because you will have reduced my price. In case I do make it, you will have really gained a lot by getting the corpse a little cheaper. Don't tell me that you think I have the same talent but because of thirty or forty pounds you're reducing my price. Does this mean that before I lost the weight, you were actually giving me thousands of dollars more for thirty globs of fat?" And I left them.

Agents were not in style when I was getting started. At that time Bill Robinson, Miss Waters, and all the stars hardly needed an agent; agents just weren't too popular then—and hardly win any "prizes of love" now. If they liked your work, owners would recommend you to other owners, and acts also recommended each other.

But this agency business has become something different. (And the agent is the one that works five days a week; we work seven.) We have almost sat back and let people destroy us. Nowadays, if you ask an actor to do an engagement, the first thing he thinks about is, "Wait a minute, I've got to find out how much tax is deductible! Is it worth leaving home for?" We have become educated to that now, and I think it's all wrong. We stop thinking about the people we're going to entertain. I thought we all were in this business to entertain people; *not* we figure first what we're going to make out of it.

Also, they tell us this is not a good job, that is not a good job, this is a lousy town, this guy's place doesn't pay much, and this and that. But is that what we came out for? And now you can't get some performers to go certain places at all. Last year I went out to Columbus, and the man asked me, "What do you want to do there? What's in Columbus?" I said, "People, about a million of them."

Once I had a show, and I asked the man to book me into someplace. And he said, "Where?" and I said, "Albuquerque." I just threw in a name, you know. He said, "Albuquerque? What are you going to do in *Albuquerque?*" I said, "They may not understand the language, but they will understand my heart. There are at least fifty thousand Navahos alone there and I'm going there to entertain them."

I once said to Bob Hope, "There's no more show love; it's just a cold, hard business." And it's true, show business has lost much of the warmth and flavor through the way it's being done today, and the people involved. So far, thank God, the real performers have been able to survive and not get too much touched by some of these things.

Bigotry never rubbed off on us before, but in show business the way it is now some people are finding ways. So far, we're keeping it out of our heads and hearts. For instance, I had something pretty crazy happen to me. I had someone say to me a couple of years ago that they wanted me to do a job, but there was a problem—a problem I had never, never heard of in show business since I'd been in it. The man said, "Pearl, there's a job and they want you; however, there is one little thing with one of the acts."

I said, "Yes?"

He said, "Well, it would be the act following you. I'll have to put it kind of candid: the problem is they're thinking it'll be two Negroes booked back to back, and they're wondering how that will be taken in the town."

It didn't exactly shock me, but I said to this man, "I have never heard anything like that in the history of show business."

He said, "Well, I haven't, either."

So I thought, "My goodness, have they really gotten this close? Are we in the theatre so surrounded by people who think like this—we who have been so pure from it for so long?"

Every field of our business now is becoming filled with people who don't have any sense of letting us be artists. It has become a dollar-sign business, and therefore we're finding it hard to do what we primarily came into it for: to be artists. Too many of us are becoming cold-hearted business people, and we're being *treated* as business people. When an artist no longer does the things that he enjoys, then he's no longer an artist.

When I began in show business, between shows we would run to each other's dressing rooms, play cards, and have laughs. Contrary to beliefs, most performers do not nip between shows.

Backstage is our home, our lives, and also should be our "privacy." It's so hard for folks to understand that. Some people think that theatrical performers ought to have lots of company backstage or in the dressing room, and even bring them to the club to socialize and mix. This backstage area is what I call our "Factory of Love." We do have to give out quite a bit of love.

Others, of the old school, which includes me, don't quite go along with having people in our dressing rooms. I learned a lot about this from brother Bill. He didn't want people in the wings while he was performing, and neither do I. Out there in the wings, the only person he wanted to see was his wife, who knew his moves and needs on the stage. She knew just when to hand him the shoes, or when to take a box full of things and walk to the wings.

Now, when you come offstage, if you have to reach for a towel from someone, or breathe, you want to see someone there who will not annoy you. Believe me, when you find someone like that (it's rare) he or she becomes your right arm.

I also learned from working with Bill Robinson once. He didn't like anyone in the wings, either. Now a lot of young performers will have many people in the wings. And these kids will find out something. That is, that you cannot entertain people in the audience and smile at them and also be entertaining people in the wings. If you see a friend in the wings, you're going to look at the audience and then you're going to look at the wings, and maybe wink your eye at your friend. You're entertaining two audiences—impossible.

In Asbury Park, between 1940 and 1943, there was a fellow on the bill named Rhythm Brown. He was standing in the wings while Bill Robinson was on and he started to talk to someone. Uncle Bo stopped the show. He called this dancer out onstage and said, "Young man, have you been on?" Right in front of the audience.

Rhythm Brown said, "Yes." He was scared to death.

Bo said, *"I'm on now,* and you learn to respect an artist when he's onstage."

I found myself doing the same thing in a more humorous way just recently. I introduced a little girl on the stage to play a guitar, and there were waiters clanking the dishes. The noise was coming primarily from the kitchen. The audience was beautiful, very, very quiet, but waiters were clanking and talking, talking over their problems, without even closing the kitchen door.

I turned on the stage and said, "Fellows, will you hold the noise down over there in the kitchen, because I have introduced an artist. If you don't, there won't be any audience to entertain, and if the audience isn't here, we won't have a job and you'll have no one to serve." The audience said, "Thank you."

Between shows I lie down on the floor most of the time. I sew or read. I don't want to entertain people then. It drains me. I want to talk only to the person who helps me in the dressing room (we have a great rapport—someone you pour the hurts out to).

You talk to this person, express things that you really can't express to any other human being. That person is an artist in her own right. She's got to know almost when to touch you and when not to touch you, to feel every move. This person must always realize that her attitude is actually your "outside curtain."

I like to leave my dressing room with a smile and good thoughts. Lois, Mickey, Dodi, Marie, Peet have helped me many years and we had a great understanding. Through some of the rough moments, they were wonderful, and I hope the same kindness was returned by me. Nothing should go onstage with you but what you're going to do, and the love of those watching you.

I don't know about other performers but between the dressing room and the stage I have what I call my moment with God, and I have passed people who wanted to speak to me, and I'd say, "Honey, not now. This is my moment with God." When you leave that dressing room, you know that you're going to have to face the people, and you don't know what to expect. I don't care whether you did a good show the first time or not, that's no guarantee for the second time.

Then I have a second moment with God when I first come off the stage. It goes way back to 1946, when the audience at the Strand welcomed me so grandly. Why some folks don't understand amazes me. It really disturbs me to come off the stage and have someone grab me and start to talk. Right then, I need that second moment with God. If it has been great, you've got to breathe and thank God. If it hasn't, you've got to think about "Lord, what did I do wrong?"

These two moments, I think, should truly belong to every performer. It's just like the cook in the kitchen. She has to have that peace while cooking. Then when the guest takes the first bite, she has to hold her breath and wonder, Is it right? Can a doctor have his mother watch the operation? It's amusing to watch the shoe cobbler. If you start to tell him *how* to fix the shoe, he'll say he's too busy and give it back to you.

It's a lucky person who can survive in this business for twenty years or more. When you reach a certain scale, there can be lots of little expenses involved in this way of life. Much is expected from you by other people; you have to try to keep things steady. I try to keep the financial side of it separate from the artistic side as much as I can. Once, a man was trying to hire me to work a club for less money, and he was flattering me. He said, "Pearl, you know, there is nobody like you." I said, "Why, listen darling, there was nobody like Edison, either—he made the electric light. In other words, you're calling me an electric bulb, but you want to pay me for candlelight." Well, it sounded pretty good at the time. At least I noticed that the manager gave up immediately.

I think it ought to be that you could work for less at particular places, if you wanted to. Say, for someone who helped you get started, or someone you like especially much, or maybe a particular club with just the right atmosphere. Wonderful Billy (Sweetpea) Strayhorn once said, "We're not in the money-making business. If we were, we'd be on Wall Street." If a man is doing what he wants inside to do, there is no real price. So why not enjoy the artistry of it? Unfortunately word gets around about your "favor of love," and you're in trouble.

Reviewers say I have a clever way of delivering asides (mumbling words). Well, true, it's one of my trademarks. I'm amused that no one has ever reasoned why. (Maybe they don't care, Pearl.) People yell to me sometimes. "We didn't hear you." I answer, "When I say something worthwhile, you'll definitely hear it. The reason I mumble, friend, is that I'm not talking to anyone but me." The question-and-answer game inside—"Should I or shouldn't I?"—makes me come up with those things you think are ad libs.

Jimmy Zito, a fine trumpet player and person, says, "Pearl, your delivery of lyrics—it's a great masterpiece." When I'm called a great "singer" I always disagree. I think of myself as telling stories to music, in tune, and the words become very important. That I love. And it doesn't hurt if you've lived a bit, too.

Dinah Washington and Nat Cole are the masters of diction. The "Queen of Song" is Ella Fitzgerald. Any questions? Singers should learn to dance. Then their phrasing would be smoother, and their body movements would synchronize with the phrasing. Some acts fall on their faces through wrong pacing. Though I'm no authority on the matter, for the younger ones who want to take a chance on Pearl, here goes. Replace tempo for tempo. If a ballad worked here last year, put one in the same spot this year. Get a good basic thing and keep it. It's always safe to open with an up tune, medium. Then stick in a ballad, or a subject-matter song, a fast one, and get off. This will at least give you a start. Oh! Throw in some talent, too.

Onstage what I give is more than what I do. The innermost is the outermost. Many performers are so cold outside they could stand a little Sterno can inside. They're too polished.

Rarely do "overnight smashes" last. Those great "recruiters of talent" always claim they've found someone new. But how many really sign new talent? Every now and then a miracle happens, like Elvis, who has outlasted most and gone on to better things, with his feet on the ground. Dean Martin has the charm of a devilish schoolboy. He's so much fun, giving all, expecting nothing but love—and he gets it.

Some of the aces are Crosby, Waters, Robinson (Bill and Sugar Ray), Hope, Benny, Horne, King Cole, Armstrong, Ellington, Sinatra, Queen Ella, Davis, Belafonte, Richman, Redman, Chevalier, Art Tatum. These folks worked hard for their success. It was not given to them on a silver platter. They're something else! I'm thankful I had a chance to see some of these people perform and meet some of them. The memory lingers on.

"Back there," we had the amateur hours to start in, and from the beginning the public had the voice about us. When the master of ceremonies came along and put his hand over the top of your head to see who won the prize, it was the *audience* that said yes or no. Today the public gets performers pushed down their throats by some enterprising "entrepreneur" (that's French). We who used to dance to the tunes of our hearts now dance to the tune of other people's heads. (We should dance *on* some of their heads.)

Stop and think. We're just people who have a talent for giving to the world. But that's no more than each human has. We happen to have a visible stage, others an invisible one. Because we are looked up to, we don't have to look down.

There was a discussion on "The Mike Douglas Show" among a group of us about whether obscene things were necessary for the stage. I felt that a man has the right to express himself, but it's not good taste to say certain words on the *stage*. Miss Waters said she agreed with me because she thinks the four-letter words destroy the dignity of the theatre. Shakespeare said, "All the world's a stage." But you've got to know which theatre you're playing at—and "know thyself." You know, the accountant stands on one stage and the actor is standing on another. Now, some people belong in a lecture hall, some people sing opera, some sing pop, some sing other things. True, you have the *right* to do anything, but is it necessarily right to do it!

While I'm going over some of the problems a performer has, I might as well mention one which has bothered me especially. The thing that really hurts is when the people you know start looking at you in a different light. You go home, and the folks look at you as though you're an oddity. They want to put a better plate on the table—you want the same plate. Really, the only place you can have that kind of natural treatment is in your own home. This is not a condemnation of people who serve you on their best china. It's a plea to leave us, please, that tiny bit of simplicity. Some stars, of course, would not agree with me. Well, sweetheart, obviously what they've achieved makes them accept falseness, and some like to give it. Who's helping whom?

People don't feel quite same way about the big performers that they used to. And the big performers don't feel the same about the people, either. Today the performer has reached the point, with television and all, of not wanting the public to touch him. They sneak out of the theatre to keep from seeing the people, you know. My Lord, years ago people used to stand at the stage door. Boy, you kept your makeup on so they could say, "Gee, she is in show business."

Some performers even work with just a tiny little spotlight and a darkened theatre throughout their act. It seems that they don't even want to see the people during the show. I had that lighting for quite a while. I worked with the darkened stage, but suddenly I just stopped. I said, "Turn up those lights!" and now I work with a pretty bright stage.

But, to tell the truth, with this new breed of show business, just so lost in themselves, it would be a relief to have the entire house go dark. It's like "Leave me alone." And they'll either wait until everybody's left the stage door, because they don't want to be bothered, or they'll just let it be known that they don't want others to touch them. They do not want humanity to come too close. In a way, we entertainers have become the untouchables of the world. I can understand some of that, too.

A lot of people think that we like being alone (and I say "we" because there are moments of this that come to all of us, and I include myself in that). But it's just that we live in glass houses, and I maintain we at least have the privilege left (I hope) of pulling the drapes.

There are also people who want us for selfish motives. We don't know who they are or where they come from. And therefore sometimes we withdraw and people misunderstand. Our friends, the ones we prefer, are the ones we've known all our lives. They are only a few. You see, the new breed of entertainer, the one since the Swing Era, is seeking someone who will call him a big shot, or who will elevate him. But for us who paid our dues (that means we worked from three dollars a week up), we want to hold on to the earth. Sure, we welcome new friends, too. Only some leave you with that question mark.

Like a balloon, you may get some helium in the head and take off. Tie some bricks to your feet, so you won't. Hold on to reality. We find these intruders coming into our lives. They may take something away from us. People ask, "What is the price of fame?" It's high: loss of privacy, loss of some friends, and the loss of some loved ones. I don't mean death loss. Sincerity gets bogged down in falseness. Your environment changes and you have to hold on to the only thing, which is *truth*.

You have talent and you've got to be awful big inside to hold on to your real self. Every human can't take going from a cloth coat to a mink coat, from rhinestones to diamonds, from a hamburger to a steak. They can't take some of the hurts that go with it, either. Take the Beatles, for instance. I look at these boys, and I say, "My God, I've never seen anything like this in my life." I was in the same hotel with them once. I'd never seen so many cops and children in my life. I don't know where they came from at two in the morning. The Beatles made many millions. I know they'd give up one of them to go outside in peace and have a meal. Who knows? They might even want a haircut by now.

So it remains for a few close old friends to know you and help you keep in touch with your real self. My dear friend Peetney Redman (Don's wife) has been real good for me that way. She knows my inside self, and how I work up for a show.

Peetney once said, "Strange, how they all think you ad lib the whole show." We were getting ready to go down and do the show at the Shoreham, in D.C. I said, touching my noodle. "I'm prepared. I prepare up above my neck [use my head]. When I go out there it looks like it's all newly made up."

Many performers do the same thing, and some do a heck of a job of trying to look unrehearsed. They look in the mirror and rehearse every smile and move. How they get fooled! The thing they think will kill the audience usually falls on its face. Then it disrupts their whole act. When someone in the audience coughs or the music goes astray, this poor creature longs to look back into her make-believe mirror and find out where all that poise went. Friend, it was never there.

I see that mirror, too, but when I go on that stage I don't see Pearl any more. I see people and they see me. I feel *them*. Once Dodi (my play daughter, now my secretary, and one of the most efficient and lovely girls in the world) started asking me what seemed like a million questions. She now is wiser, but at that time she was young and I was impatient at teaching the young. (Forgive me, children.) One day after what seemed the five hundredth question, I said, "Stop asking so much."

She replied, "My father told me if I didn't know, I should ask."

I said, "Did he ever tell you to use your other senses, too? Observe sometimes and you may see the answer; or listen, and you may hear it before you ask. And look at the breath you'll save." I continued. "Dodi, life is like music—one, two, three, four—but you must remember to put that breath in between."

Folks, there's a pause: ask the musicians. Otherwise, where's the rhythm? Dodi can still ask questions, but oh brother! has she learned some beautiful answers (with rests in between). I remembered this bit because I told the story to a fine girl, Dorothy Shay, and Dottie tried to make me name this book "Life Is One and Two and . . ."

I often think it's like a sporting house. If you work in a sporting house and somebody calls and says, "Hey, I've got a hundred-dollar trick for you," you're very likely to go. That's the way some performers work. First, "How much?" I always felt that I had my *own* sporting house in show business. It's not an ordinary one, though. One night I might decide that's the night I'm giving it away free for fun. Then when the rent comes due I would charge and still have fun. Each time I would give, receive, and enjoy. A man cannot price his talents except in joy.

The genuine performers are all in the business for the artistry of it. They are in it for the love of that public, for the warmth. The legends are those who are more than performers. They have never stopped being human beings.

8

I've read so many books where the authors are busy complaining about the effects of racial prejudice on their lives. There have been other people who've had troubles but kept forging ahead. To them should go some credit for their many hurts and continued efforts. I ask the complainers, "When did you become so aware of these things, before or after you attained what you desired?" These terrible things that happen should bring more than just tears. Me, I like people and have always felt that I belong and you belong. We are all God's. Inside and out I don't feel any different from anyone else. Much of what I see I don't like, but I don't like it for anyone—purple or green. (Just thought I'd change colors for the novelty.)

The prejudiced people can't insult you because they're too blinded by their own ignorance. When you think of Jewish people pushed into ovens or made into lampshades, you have to be thankful. Folks don't think enough of you to put you in their home as a "brown skin lampshade." How fortunate you are!

Yet we do some pretty terrible things to each other. An

amusing thing happened on a USO trip to Brownsville, Texas, which gave me a little touch of some Southern hospitality from the side I least expected. The trains were always late at this time, what with the troop movements, and most of the time the Army reception committee was later than the train. I would get pretty hungry before I could get off the train and find a meal.

That day I was hungrier than ever, and right across the street from the station I spied not one but two restaurants. As soon as I crossed the street, I could see why there were two. One was marked "White" and one "Colored." (At this point I didn't quite realize how important these signs were down there.) I started into the colored one and two ladies stopped me, on their way out. "Honey, you'll have to go someplace else. I'm closing," this lady said, as she backed me out. We all started explaining to her how long we had to wait for the Army, and that we were also new in town and knew of no place to go. She told us no deal. She had to go to the hairdresser. We said we'd take a sandwich to eat outside, and this child still said, "But, baby, I've got to get my hair fixed." Now ask yourself, who's to blame for that?

She locked her door and left.

We sat over at the station, angry at her and slowly starving, we thought. There was big talk of going across the street to the other place, but no one made the move. Courageous Pearl took matters in hand (and, may I add, life, for how did I know what would occur?). The others told me how dangerous it was, but I felt I might just by chance run into a human being. When I entered the white restaurant, the entire place turned. A voice said, "We don't serve—" but that's as far as she got.

I said, "I know you don't, but give me food and I'll take it out."

The woman looked at me and said, "Sit down at that stool on the end and eat."

Sitting on the end couldn't hurt my feelings. It was the only seat left. Now my friends came peeping in the window making signs which I could read clearly but paid no attention to: bring a coke, bring a sandwich. I thought, "The hell with them. Suppose my throat had been cut. They would have been hungry and I would have been mighty dead."

In September 1952, an incident happened that could have changed my whole life in many ways, mentally and physically. A distaste for humanity could have soured me for life. All the things I read each day of horrors committed for racial reasons recall to me what I might have become. Fear was not the cause of my overcoming what happened to me. It was the supreme knowledge that good will prevail. I'm not one who waits on man, but one who knows that Fate carries its own clock.

A friend, Jeanie Terrell, and I went to the Riviera in New Jersey to see Frank Sinatra's show and afterwards waited for the room to clear before leaving. Many of the waiters knew me from my having worked clubs in New York, and they talked to me. Finally, we started through the lobby, where a group of men were standing. The ladies must have gone to the powder room. A man pulled my jacket and said, "Come here, Sarah." (Too bad Sarah, Mandy, and Liza sound so appropriate to call certain folks. How sad and ignorant.)

I kept walking, hoping he would turn me loose, but he held on and I was pulled backward. He repeated, "I said, come here." When he gave that second jerk, it brought me back far enough for him to push me against the wall. He said, "I said, Sarah, come here and I meant it," all the while drawing back his fist.

All I could see was a sea of faces, sadistic faces. As that big fist started toward my face, Jeanie (bless her) must have hit at him with her purse or something, because he whirled, and I ran back into the club, calling to Jeanie, "Let's go this way." I heard footsteps and hoped Jeanie and I could make it, although I didn't know for sure where the back door led or even where it was. There was only one thing in my mind—to escape these creatures. Incidentally, in the few moments the lobby scene took, I recall seeing some feminine faces. Boy, would you believe a female could watch another one being treated like that! (We are the deadliest of the species.)

When I got backstage I heard someone say, "Heh." I turned and, pow, I went spinning around like a top. At that time I had a small bridge in my mouth and it was knocked out, I assure you, more quickly than the dentist had put it in. I hit the floor. It was dark and frightening. There was no place to run anymore. I was in a corner alone with this face of hate.

If I didn't get up, I was done for, but every time I did he'd knock me down and kick me in my stomach. He was trying to kill me. I prayed, and, folks, God answers prayers. I knew I was going down for the last time when a voice said, "What are you doing to this girl?" Then two men were fighting like crazy. It seems that the last waiter to leave had heard the commotion. His glasses were broken and his face cut, I later heard, but the man who had been punching me ran. May I thank the man who saved me now, wherever he is, and most of all for giving me a reason not to hate everyone.

The waiter got help and took me upstairs to an office. He called the owner, Bill Miller, who immediately came back from New York. He was furious, and called the police and the doctor. My ears were cut and bleeding, my jaw sore, and my stomach bruised. The police kept pounding on one thing, "Were they white men?" I told them I didn't give a dern if they were purple, they had struck an innocent person and I wanted them caught. For the sake of the curious, yes, they were white. But they represented for me *all* the miserable people of the world who go around looking at Skin. I often wonder when I read of folks who treat human beings like dogs, who stomp on them and kill them, who or what are they hitting? How could a man hate someone he had never met before, just because he had a different color skin? What is he really afraid of?

They worked on the case for two years, but to no avail. There is one compensation. The man who did this must live with himself, and it can't be easy. How many times he has to look in his mirror and see how ugly he is.

A nice friend, Saki. sat and took care of me, read to me during the next few days as I lay there in pain. The papers wrote editorials on the cruelty inflicted on me, and I sup-

Papa

Mama

Pearl Bailey at the age of three

"The One and Only" Bill Bailey

Eura with Tony Bellson

Virgie

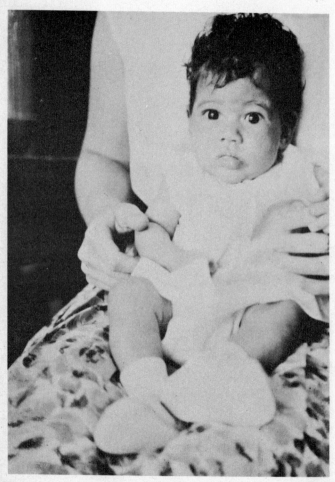

Dee Dee Bellson at four months

Pearl Bailey and Sammy Davis, Jr., in a scene from *Porgy and Bess*

Josephine Premice, Diahann Carroll, Pearl Bailey, and Juanita Hall in *House of Flowers*

Pearl Bailey and Nat King Cole on set of *St. Louis Blues*

Pearl Bailey in kitchen on ranch at Apple Valley, California, taken during filming of *Porgy and Bess* in 1958

Pearl, Louie, and Tony Bellson at Las Vegas airport

Bill Avery

Eura, Mrs. Bellson, Pearl, Louie, and Tony in Las Vegas

Pearl Bailey onstage at the Flamingo in Las Vegas

Pearl Bailey, Joe Louis, and the Valenzuela boys in Las Vegas

Pearl Bailey and Don Redman at a recording session

Pearl Bailey at her fiftieth birthday party, with "Peetney" Redman

posed with a little pushing there could have been a full-scale riot worked up. Many thoughts of revenge crossed my mind, I'll admit. But I just lay there. Saki kept reading, I kept aching, and, gentlemen, you just keep remembering.

During my third stint at the Beverly Hills Country Club in Newport, Kentucky, one of the bosses asked me where my next job was. I told him Vegas, and he said he would see me there around the hotel. I told him I doubted if he'd see me, since they did not let the brown-skin acts stay there. Either he was surprised or he was a damn good actor. He asked where we stayed and I told him on the "west side." Long before, I had started thinking of this area of Vegas as beyond an iron curtain.

It was wild to ride down the main street, go under the viaduct into absolute darkness. The wild dogs would run behind the cars like Jesse James and a band of robbers. They had gambling and the joints were jumping, but, part-ner, it was dark—unpaved streets and shacks. Still, down there lots of money was changing hands among the gamblers. I've never seen so many Cadillacs in front of shacks in my life, and quite a few big bills crept out of over-all pockets. Mrs. Harrison and Mrs. Shaw kept the show people. I stayed with Mrs. Harrison and cooked there.

Well, when I told him about this, the man in New-port said, "You have just as much right as anyone to stay where it's nice." I knew it, too. Any time people pay you fabulous money, why the hell don't they think you could afford a better room? I didn't make an issue of it. I'm not averse to staying anyplace that's nice and clean. What the heck! People are people. He told me this time the hotel would have a place, but when I arrived, well, someone was mixed up (as per usual). Did I have a stroke? No! I merely mentioned to my employer that I had not gotten my usual room because this room at the hotel was supposed to be there, so he went to work and found a place. They called the local gift shop, and the people who had it were moving into a fine house right in back of the club. They were show people, and they were moving in that day. They said, "Great! We'd love to have her." (Lord love show folks!)

Another time I was working in Chicago on the bill with

Joey Bishop—crazy! There is a funny and sweet man. One night while I was there, a girl named Fay and I decided on an Oriental meal. (At this period of my life, I must say I dined quite heavily—and it showed.) Now, Chicago had queer ideas about who went where, but that was far from my mind. Somewhere I read, "Trouble comes threefold: first, in anticipation; second, it happens; third, you worry how did it start." So I wear no chips, and get no splinters before my time.

Off we went to this restaurant, imagining a huge dinner and relishing every morsel in advance. As we walked in, the man at the door threw a fast word at us in his language and pointed upstairs. Up we went, for it was rather crowded below. We found an empty booth (what a stroke of luck), and as we looked at the elaborate menu we enlarged our meal. The reading of the menu was great, but we waited a long time to give the order. After a half hour, a bell rang in our skulls. No service. By now, of course, we were so hungry we couldn't have walked out if we had tried. All strength was gone. A waiter came by on his mission, and I once more gave the signal and he again waved me off.

Suddenly, I stood up, and he bumped into me on his way back. He started with the language I couldn't understand, but he kept ending with "Me no serve."

That did it. I told him in a slow Oriental drawl, "You think I came to America to pick cotton. I was told you came to do laundry, so, brother, serve." And you know what? He did.

In later years I was in that place again, and they were so in love with me I could have taken a slow boat to China and been the only brown one eating with chopsticks. I guess after thinking over what I'd said, it dawned on them that here was simply a hungry woman.

We have reached a point in our history where we can no longer delay our plans to do right. There is much hatred, deceit, and corruption practiced—all humanity must put on the chains of love and forge them to themselves until we can no longer shake off love.

There are about fifteen Constitutions. Wouldn't it be

much better to follow the original one? Think how much paper we'd save and how right we could be. The rewrites are getting so frequent that soon we'll forget where we started—then find out we never did. How can you give a man a room in a house and not let him come through the front door? What's on the welcome mat: Who are you? What are you?

In some ways we should all be displeased with ourselves. We must begin to take hold before we destroy ourselves, our inner selves—our morality. Some of the liberals—of all races—are all talk and no action. They have to have a membership card before they can think or act.

The horrors north, south, east, and west should be spared the entire nation. It's all a disgrace. The main streets of the North are becoming more like the backwoods of the South. The North has merely lived under a thin veil of liberalism.

People in general could take a lesson from those who are in the theatre. There's a beautiful understanding among people in the theatre; we have no chips on our shoulders, no burdens to carry, because we all have a thing in common, a cause. Of course, there are people leading various crusades today. Suddenly, there's a lot of leading. Many people are following and haven't quite made up their minds where they're being led. That's something I never wanted.

Has anyone likened this problem to a bird coming out of an egg? His emerging is slow but at one point suddenly he pops out, looks around and is unafraid.

The man who is really afraid is the one who has been out and now is being closed into the eggshell. Pity him—he doesn't know how dark it is in there. Let us start to think not just of race—or religion or creed—but in terms of a complete life. Shall we walk with "Labels of Fear"? I deny no group anything. We all belong to each other.

How can I lead my brother down a path when I'm stumbling myself? Let us all take up the struggle. Make wide the path so we can all go through. Shall I pick the yellow daffodils and leave the red rose because it has thorns? Shall I take one brother and leave the other?

The Negro's face has become sullen because of these

awful things, but we cannot be proud and self-righteous, either. The Negro problem in America certainly is not the only problem we have. We should be displeased with the Indian problem in America—the "Humanity" problem. We have all helped to wipe the smiles from the Indian's face. Who gave anyone all these privileges? No one! How dare we?

Years ago in the neighborhoods, children would skip by and call each other names, but that's about as far as it went. At least they weren't beating each other up in the neighborhoods as they're doing nowadays, without a word. Man started this horrible thing, and man will have to see it through God's eye before it ends.

Someone asked me on the Mike Douglas TV show whether I "marched." I said, "No, I haven't marched any-place physically, but I march every day in my heart. I live with humanity every day, and when you live with humanity then you have walked—and the road is not easy, necessarily."

People are so quick to point out the favors a Negro gets because he is an entertainer. We have paved the way for many, and, too, have paid with blood, sweat, and tears. Which is worse—being damned for the paint job of your skin, or being praised for your talents and pushed up on a pedestal for all mankind to see while the wolves howl at the base of the statue? I wonder.

Don't you think we as artists cry for help? Are you all so deceived by that spotlight? Sure we get, but we also give. The hunger, the cold flat, the unemployment—it's all ours, too. We pay our debts as we go. If you have so decided, to live on an installment plan, then it is up to you to figure out how to pay the mortgage. No one can figure out your worth but you. Then forge ahead. Why stand in the line that's marked "bus stop" when you're actually waiting for a cab?

Self-consciously, Negroes have started to shun certain jobs. People say, "Don't do this. They're using you as they have through the years." Sure, at one point there were Negro trades, but over the years they have become the trades of everyone. I thoroughly agree that folks should be offered more than jobs as maids, cooks, or porters, but each man, regardless of his race, should be offered something only when he is capable of doing the work. If you are not capable of doing something, you're going to get fired anyway. To take a person who is not capable, be he of whatever race, and put him in a position he can't handle is to do him much more harm than good. Open the doors so people can become prepared.

In the present day there's the big issue about using Negro performers in television. The industry has been trying to give Negroes a better chance to get started, but it looks sort of silly. Now what do you see? There's a play and there's a colored couple dancing in the room. They have fifty white couples, but there's the one couple just dancing in the room, and somehow they never make a mistake and dance with anyone else but each other. A sponsor once asked me, "Would it pay off to advertise hair products to Negroes?" What a stupid question. Sure! What does he think? Does he suppose that Negro women run around with dirty, greasy hair? Come out of it, honey, grow up. Learn something about people.

In TV you're told, "We'd love to have you, but the sponsor [or the South] won't buy it." You know, what makes this whole thing so silly is the fact that most of the products advertised today have been used for years by those whom they call the "servants in the house." But for a commercial on TV they get someone with a fifty-dollar permanent and a diamond ring saying, "I use such-and-such a product to clean my sink and to scrub the walls." That's ridiculous! Why not use some of the people that have done this work for years? At least it would look more authentic.

In November 1965, I did a TV spectacular. The following May, a fan wrote a letter: "You're spectacular!" In the first of the letter was a little rhyme that said, "I'm not a Negro or a Jew, but I sure like you . . ." And it went on and on to praise me. I usually jot down on the envelope what I want to say for an answer, then send it over to my secretary, Dodi. Well, when she got it, she called me and said, "Mama [that's what she calls me], what do I say to this person?" Now, Dodi happens to be of the Hebrew faith. I said, "Darling, you should know how as well as I do, because you're in there, too. In this way, this person is telling you that, though he doesn't approve of either Negroes or Jews, I sure got a break, because I'm one exception to the rule. So actually he thinks he's praising us." I said, "You just write back and tell him that I received the letter and understand his thoughts, but I've become so involved with the human race I never had time to find out what a man was before I liked him."

Listening to some people saying, "We're doing fine," I said, "Yeah, you're doing fine, you really think you're making it." They said, "Oh yes, you know they're using Negroes all in television and everything." I said, "That's right, just like the painting of the Lord's Supper. The Thirteenth Disciple—they painted him on. There's no chair for him. He's still serving the dinner." I say this without any malice toward anyone. It's just amusing to me that everybody is so deceived.

Sometimes I stop and think that today we are in many ways losing as a nation. The race problem is only one thing we have to solve. We are disliked in so many lands—it's fantastic.

I wasn't going to get into this in this book, but the world is into it now. Why are they now passing so many different laws? We don't need anything else. We have one Constitution. Where in the world are we going to put all the papers we're making up? We don't have a building in Washington large enough to stack up all these new laws. Somebody's got to throw the paper away—and literally they do. It's like signing something and laying it by an open window and letting the wind blow it away. It's so strange that the war I thought we won, we really lost—the Revolutionary War. I thought in 1776 they said that was it, the *one,* when they got a piece of paper called Constitution.

Everyone wants to do something to help, but nobody wants to be the first. It's like collecting social security; nobody wants to go down and get the social-security check because the lady next door might be down getting hers. Nobody wants the neighbors to know that he got a check and that's how he got the new dining-room furniture. But he should show his dining-room furniture and say, "Look, honey, look what the government gave me. It's my money, and I got it back and bought a dining-room set." Same thing with love and truth—it's all yours, friend. Make the most of it.

Each man wants to wait. Each man wants to send a telegram of support but stay safely distant. But you cannot always telegraph your thoughts, and I think that's where a lot of trouble's coming from. James Meredith walked, you know.

Every man wants to lose his fear. I certainly think he has a right to lose his fear, because that's something that can destroy anyone. Each of us has a certain fear. We don't admit it. Many are asking, "How do we get rid of fear?" Well, first we have to do exactly what Mr. Meredith did, walk down the road and lose it on our own. I don't think anyone could do it for a man better than he can do it himself. When Meredith fell, some of our dignity as a nation fell with him. Thank God he arose.

Love your neighbor, and never mind so much instructing. Understanding is going to have to come from love, and the basic truth. We have to get it from within. But we must use that force within not as a destructive power but as a constructive power. The way we're going to get understanding is for each man to open his heart and open his mind and look within himself as he looks at his neighbor.

I say these things not as a politician, not as an organizer, not as a Communist, not as anything. But we heard the Russians say years ago that they would never put an army against us, they would let us destroy ourselves from within. Suddenly we seem to be doing what someone else had planned for us instead of what we planned for ourselves.

I was riding along in a certain city recently, and as I was riding I looked out the window of the cab. I saw boarded-up houses and people lying in the street. I was going through different neighborhoods, seeing different groups. The scene started to change, and I got to thinking. The cab driver happened to be a quiet one, and that ride gave me one of my few quiet moments. Suddenly, just as I got to my destination, I thought, "Why is every man leaving his own house to clean up somebody else's when each man needs to clean his own?" Each person in America today could, should, and must contribute to the ideal of freedom—complete freedom. You agree with that? Then let him have a house of his choosing, where he chooses, and see.

Tony Bennett once said to me, "Pearl, you have no neuroses." He had come backstage to the dressing room at the Cocoanut Grove to talk to me. I said, "I have no false pride. I have dignity. A man is born with dignity." I always like the expression which says, "You can be a queen in an alley." I have seen people in an alley. That's why I don't buy some of the things that are going on now. I have seen clean curtains at the window and a clean yard. The one next door may have trash and everything may be dirty, including the children. Because people are in an alley, that does not take away their class. Maybe economically they can't get out. Maybe they have many reasons, but that does not take away their dignity. And when they come home at night, they have every right to hold their heads as high as the man who is living on Main Street, who could be the biggest bum in the world.

People should stop pigeonholing other people. I remember in 1948 I ran across something in England which bothered me. I'm not the lord of all the English language, and I use my hands for words sometimes, but I certainly do not talk in dialect. It burns me up when I have an interview and then pick up the paper the next day and the interview is in dialect. It's not "the" manager, it's "de" manager. Gentlemen, I would love for you to do one thing for me. Whatever your question, I don't mind answering it, but whatever you write, I do wish you would write it, not maybe in your King's English, but for heaven's sake write it in American English. Amazing grace, I did return recently—no dialect. Could be a sign of growth or listening better?

Of course, the English don't have too high an opinion of the way we're handling our problems, but they have one of the greatest of all race problems, I think, with their West Indian people, the people from their islands. In 1948 I saw people who looked like dogs lying in the street. They had ship's ropes around their waists to hold their pants up.

Also the Hebrew people were discussed there as you might discuss the colored problem here. They can say the word "Jew" so it sounds like mud. What is wrong with man? Sometimes I think he's going to hell at one hundred miles an hour.

Some say belonging to nothing you sit back and watch. I say by belonging to humanity I care, friend. I don't have to join an organization to care. I care about *everyone*, and that's more important than caring about one.

It's said, "Sure, people should live together. They should eat and do these wonderful things together." But I've noticed that every time a Negro moves into one of these neighborhoods two-thirds of the people move out, and pretty soon you know what you've got? You have another slum neighborhood all over again, and now that Negro who moved in has got to go someplace else to find a decent place to live. But ask—who's running?

There's a saying, "No man is an island." Yet how many of us accept that lonely place, "our little island," in our minds, closed in on all sides by our own selfishness and hurts, closed in with our personal feelings against our fellow man. How wonderful it would be if every human would make up his mind to be just a small peninsula. If only we could put a small strip of land on the edge of this island we've created, it might reach the mainland. At least we would have started for reality. Before long we would find little patches of land stretching from all sides. No longer would we be alone.

The following was written around seven one morning long after the first part of this chaper. I had a worrisome revelation* in my sleep, so I present it now, knowing it will bother you, too—and I hope for the good.

BARE THE BACKS FOR THE LASH

Listen my children, my children, and you shall hear crying. The whip has cut the flesh open; salt is being poured into the wound. It's going to burn and ache. Will it hurt as much as it did many years ago? Did you expect a softer whip? Were you prepared for all the blows? Are these new wounds? Will they bleed more? Can they hit harder now? Whose place to lead, whose to follow? Where did it all go wrong? Where was it ever right? Who is to blame and who is left to care? Did we run too fast—or too slow? Where does the race end? Where is the finishing tape? Who sits in the judge's box? Is he right or wrong? How many contestants have dropped out? How many were in the race? What do we do now? Where do we go? If we win what do we lose, and if we lose what do we win? What is the prize? Is it of value to us? Who sponsored the race? Where is he? What is he? True or false? Is he still there holding the laurel wreath? Is it made of flowers or thorns? When they announced me winner, did I gloat or pray? Have I invited joy or sorrow?

It seems so long ago that people declared, "Let us be free." Was it the Romans, Greeks, Jews, Egyptians —who was it who first said that? Who answered No? Was it the Philistines, Germans, Africans? Have we ever been free? I doubt it, because we would not have put back on again the bonds of hatred, of Master and Servant.

What happened to the "Brother Outfit"? Did you become filled with the idea that no tailor could make a "Suit of Love" to fit you? Did you not want to wear it because you feared friends might laugh? Well, coward friend, it's not a new style at all. It came out thousands of years ago, and man kept altering it to suit his tastes, because to him it has never fitted just right. Why not go back to the original pattern; it was cut from good cloth, elasticized so it could fit all. After you put it on, look into the mirror of your heart (wipe it clean first). See if it isn't pretty.

Backlash, frontlash—it all hurts. Time will prove that strongly. The hand of Fate is open and we can stand firmly within. I have watched the victors smile. It was not sweet. I watched the losers smile. It was not happy. Why? Because each one was still puzzled at the final outcome. When they arrived at the post, false judges had moved the tape, and the True Judge was gone. Some of the friends were there. So were some of the enemies of both the winners and the losers.

What do you know! After using all that time and energy, the race has to be run again. Why? Because, dear ones, it was not a single man's race but a relay. It was handing the Torch of Freedom to each member of each team continuously. It was not how fast we ran but, rather, setting a steady pace and keeping it. The trick was making sure the torch got into your brother's hand.

The flame is not out. Rekindle it with understanding. Worry not about those who said, "I poured water on it. I'm sure it's out." How many times has it been thought the fire was out and it still smoldered? That is the worst kind of fire, when it ignites again. Make sure it is to burn a long time. Pour on the kerosene of Faith. And it will last. Make sure you don't set it so close to your fellow man that he will burn, nor so far that he cannot be warmed.

Listen my children and you shall hear laughter. The whip has cut the flesh, the salt has been poured in, but the wound will heal. The hand that holds the whip may sometimes have more sores from gripping the handle than the back that receives the lash. Bare the back! Grasp the whip! Which are you? What will you win? What will you lose?

Backlash, Frontlash, take off your false garments. There's something behind you—Time and Truth.

Something else I want to include here, written by a dear friend who calls himself my son, and I'm proud. We compare and discuss poetry, music, and life. Pete must be twenty-one now. Actually he's the son of Eleanor Powell and Glenn Ford. He said I could use his poem. I get goose pimples from it.

LIFE

That was the day I first saw wholly new
The confusion of souls on this planet of ours.
People mature and live their lives,
Cheat and steal till the day they die.
Even animals survive as the fittest can,
Although their pattern was started when the world
*   began.*
But was this the life which was meant to be?
Suffering, confusion, scorn, do these constitute reality?
Life will continue, needless to say,
Until someone, somewhere, will show them the way.
Think, if some beautiful unknowing thing
Should unfortunately view the state that we're in—
What if a rose should enter God's scheme,
A rose which is purity to its utmost extreme?
It would lift its petals high and wide,
Look around and observe,
Wilt, and die.

His way of looking at some of the cruel things in the
world is so beautiful for one who must have been about
sixteen when this was written. I haven't met his father
yet, but Mama is a great performer. Putting Pete's poem
in the book and not Mama's wouldn't be quite fair since
they both fit the subject so well. Ellie wrote this. It shows
the soul of a woman you watched many years on the screen.

OUTSIDE THE SPECTRUM

Our heavenly father must have loved
The colors . . . every one,
For he scattered them upon the earth,
From pastel rainbow spun.
Across the dome of heaven
To the sea's deep changing hue,
He made the brown earth, trees of green,
The summer sky of blue.
The sunset blaze, the afterglow,

The dawn diffused in rising mist,
The mountains' purple aureole,
The morning glories dewdrop kissed.
But when he looks on man I think
He sees but soul and mind;
And where his children are concerned
Our father's color-blind.

9

It's hard to accept strength and goodness together in the same person. When we find it, we say, "What's the matter with him. Is he afraid?" We wonder, "Why doesn't he hit back at the world?" I know one such person. He has never talked about it, but I believe way back, when he was a small boy, people around him showed evil and cruelty. He probably decided then, "I'll never be like that."

I'm talking about my husband, Louis Bellson, the great drummer, the Louis I have mentioned several times already. We have been married for sixteen years very happily. But it was not easy for me to find this kind of relationship. And since I have known unhappiness in marriage, I can appreciate the more what Louis and I have.

Around August or September of 1952, I went to California to work, and of course stayed at Rose's. We were sitting in the kitchen, chitchatting away on our theories of life. Rose said, "I know you've had your romantic disappointments in life, but there's no need to refuse to go out on dates at all."

I told her that I was not much of a socializer (believe

me, I'm not). I used to come from work, whether playing a club or making a picture, eat my meal, read, play
records or just talk with Mrs. Brown (who by then was
about eighty). Rosie started telling me about this nice young
fellow who was working with Juan. Juan was with Duke
Ellington. They also worked with Harry James, and every
time they played the Coast, this "nice young man" stayed
with them. What struck her fancy, and Juan's, was the character of this musician. Rose thought that he and I were
similar in many ways.

I said, "Dear Rosie, I do not even care to discuss anyone romantically."

That was not her idea; she was just pleased when she
found people in the theatre interested in something else
than "living it up" all the time. "Thank goodness," she
said, "we have a breed of show folk now who want home
life, too." This conversation went no further and was forgotten. My next job was in Washington, D.C., where Juan
would also be working, but first I went home to New York.

I was on my way to Washington to play the Kavokas
Club, then off to Europe. They did not feature tablecloths
and such at the Kavokas, but I was given the royal treatment, with a cloth and a rose on each table.

Before leaving for the club, I dropped over to the backstage of the Howard Theatre to speak to Juan and tell him
that Rosie had been well when I left her. As I drove up,
Juan was just crossing from the restaurant where the show
people ate and came to the car to give me a peck on the
cheek. After we talked, I started to pull off. But when someone said, "Hi, I'm Louie," I turned and there was a smiling
face; so I answered, "I'm Pearl." Juan and Louie came
to see the show that night, and afterward we got some food.
The next day I had a poem and an orchid. (Love in
bloom!) Luigi Balassoni was a drummer, a nice fellow, and
he was the guy whom Rose had wanted me to meet.

I lived at Edwina's across from the theatre. I know very
few show folks who haven't stayed there. I'd known her
about sixteen years, and she'd been in business for ages.
All of us played tonk (the card game), ate, slept, and had
a ball. I had a little girl with me named Sally. She called

me Mama. Sally lived on 126th Street when it was at its worst, so it was nice to be able to get her out of that environment. She used to sit on the steps of her house back of the Apollo Theatre and wait for me to call her for errands. I was very attached to her. Happy to say, she continued on to nice things in life.

Edwina was a grand old lady of sixty-one or more, and still swinging. There were about twenty rooms in that house, and she saw to it that they were immaculate. Her prices were reasonable, and she was an exceptional cook. Today her daughter Julia Mae is a dietician in a famous place in Chicago. But neither she nor I could ever keep up with Mom Wina.

Three nights after we met, Louie, Duke, Harry James, and Mom came to the club. Oh! She kept up with the gang, loved her beer, and would dance at the drop of a hat. She'd rag out in gorgeous clothes, bedecked with diamonds (she had a cigar box full), and off she'd go.

Marion Bruce, a dance act, chorus line, and Pearl: that was the show. Louie doesn't drink, so he sat and nursed a glass of wine all night. (For family reunions he'll finish a glass.) Edwina told me during the show she had turned to look at him and he was watching me so intently that she asked what he thought.

He said, "Fascinating, just fascinating."

On the fourth night, when I went in, Marion and Sally told me I looked in love, and they said, "That guy's in love with you." When Louie came that night, he asked me to step outside after the first show, because he wanted to talk about something personal. We sat in my car across the street, and Lou said, "You know, we're closing, and I want to ask you a question."

I said, "I know you do."

He said, "You know what the question is . . ."

I said, "Yes."

He said, "Then if you know what it is, what is the answer?"

I said, "Well, I'll tell you. Do you know what it will involve?"

He said, "Yes, I do."

I said, "Yes is the answer."

He said, "But I was getting ready to say would you marry me?"

I said, "I've already answered you."

And that's all that's ever been said, ever, about our marriage being something different.

Louis was going on some one-nighters before joining me in England. I had opened in London at the Colony Club and was awaiting the arrival of my love one night when I heard a knock at the door, and the waiter handed me a thick telegram. Oh, it was terribly thick. He kept telling me the photographers were outside. And I said, "What are they doing out there?"

I looked, and there was just a mess of them outside my dressing-room door. Louis' father had sent a wire to the press saying, "My son is marrying out of the race." But he didn't make a lot of it; it wasn't cruel. It was sad because he was confused as to the race issue and pressure of people in his town, poor man. It was funny, because he didn't know whom to wire, so he had sent this telegram to the Associated Press, and I mean all of them were there at my door.

One of them said to me, "What do you think about this?" This was my well-known reply, "There is only one race, the human race." The world, I hope, will never forget that one line because I meant it.

Now the excitement was building; there was no rest now. The English people had made this a Cinderella story, and I've never seen so many cameras and photographers anywhere, that night and later.

Lou had been appearing with Duke Ellington, at the Paramount Theatre in New York. Duke gave him two weeks off to come to London for the wedding. I was waiting at the airport for Lou, along with about thirty or forty newspaper writers and photographers. They say there were more there than at Anthony Eden's wedding. They kept asking me how they would know him, so they could race out as soon as the plane landed. I told them, "The first person who gets off the plane smiling, that's Louie."

Finally, the plane was sighted, off they went, and, sure

enough, there was a guy coming down the stairs smiling as usual at the world.

Lou told me later how he saw all the people and kept looking around the plane for the big celebrity. He had no knowledge of the wire that had been sent, or that because of a big jazz tune, "The Hawk Talks," which he had written for Harry James, the musicians had turned out in mass. Nor did I know he was so popular over there.

Don't think that I'm gushing like a silly schoolgirl. I've been, as you've read, married before. But my other marriages are far in the unhappy past. I feel like this: One day I was house-cleaning my life, lifted the rug and saw dirt (mental and physical), so decided to clean up. I swept up quite a bit, and put it in the trash can of the past. Each human being has lived, and if he lifts his rug he, too, will see dirt, and so he can at least appreciate the fact I've tried to straighten my house.

There are people who could really be hurt if I went into too much detail about my past. We should deliver no pain. A professor in Midland, Michigan, told me a beautiful thing when I told him I was writing a book: "Give something to the world to help." And I shall do just that and nothing more. So our wedding is beauty, and it's something to give to you all. We love sharing.

When "Smiley" got off the plane and all the guys were snapping away, we were hysterical with laughter, and many people seeing this picture in America thought, "Look at those two jazz fiends acting silly."

No one ever knew what we were giggling about. But before Lou came, he called and asked if I wanted him to bring any food. England was still short of food, and I had a small kitchen, so I suggested some corn-meal mix. I had plenty to eat, but Louie was such a huge eater, a little more food wouldn't hurt. He had this big brown paper bag under his arm, and here was all this glitter and glamour going on, and Customs never even asked this man from a foreign shore what was in that big bag. That was pretty wild, because they were very strict about what you could bring into the country. That photograph is still my favorite picture, and I take it everyplace.

There was a three-day waiting period after getting the license, and Lou was happy over that because his trunk had not arrived, and he only had a suède jacket and brown pants. The Colony Club was so formal. No one was allowed in without the grand tuxedo, but they let Louie in. I think with all that publicity, and the place being jammed, they would have let him in naked. Everyone was coming to see the Cinderella Story in action.

Wednesday morning, we started out for Caxton Hall (the same as City Hall) in a Rolls-Royce that had been sent by someone. Pearl (the friend helping me in the dressing room), Ernie Anderson (another friend), Louie and I were enjoying our high-class trip when the car came to a sudden halt. There in the middle of the street was a mob of people, so thick that there was no way to move another inch. Bands were playing "The Hawk Talks"; newsreel cameras were on top of the buildings; it was complete bedlam. Everyone was cheering and dancing from sheer joy. It was misinterpreted at home as a wild party or something. It was a thing of beauty. The English meant it. They all tried to get into the building, which was impossible. Marie Bryant Azariah, her darling husband John, who signed the license, Patterson and Jackson, Lloyd Phillips, all were shedding tears of happiness. The registrar's name was J. Doomsday Holiday.

For the next week people walked down the street behind us, just smiling. They showed the wedding in the movies. We were like the Pied Piper with all the children following.

Besides working the Colony, I also worked the second show at the Astor in the same building. One night, we went to see *Porgy and Bess,* with our little crowd going with us as far as the box office. I went back then for my second show, and the two stars of *Porgy* came down to the club. I called on the young lady to sing a song. She did, and upset the entire place. Such a voice was not to be believed! Later it was truly heard. She was a girl who became world famous, Leontyne Price. Of course William Warfield (her husband at that time and a great singer) sang marvelously, too. We had quite a ball in dear old

London Town. Al Burnett's, Seigi Sessler's, Churchill's were the swinging spots then.

Louis and I have found a beautiful level. Now I find, after all the ups and downs, the real self, "the raw Pearl," coming out. I can look back on the unsteady times and understand some of them and in time will understand more. I had always been looking for something more in my life and I guess for a while I was just too ready to think I'd found it.

If you're lonely or despondent, after creating for yourself a million nonexistent problems, any gaiety you find will carry you off, sometimes into a path of falseness. At the time it looks well lit all the way. Only when you've traveled a distance do you see the darkness there. Sometimes in my happiness now, I feel I must never have lived those other experiences, but how else would I have learned? Sometimes it's like a dream. Growing up is what it really is. I sought things, and Lawdy! I found them. Many turned out so wrong, but then I didn't go into them right. I can only hope each person I knew back then was not harmed too much.

A marriage of two showmen is looked on as impossible, but that's not so: you have lots in common. And if you keep respect for each other's individuality, there's no danger. Oh, you clash like any other married couple, but your work can take you out of that quickly sometimes.

Louis said to me when we were married, "I'm not particular about your working. However, you're a great artist, and I would be less than right to ask you to give up something God has given you." He also added, "The day you want to stop, do and it will be fine. I'll take care of you."

Louis, I didn't tell you then, but that's the first time that statement had been made since I had left Mama's door. Thanks, sweetie, and as the years go on you will notice I'm taking advantage of that statement, and you're living up to your word. What more can a female ask? We have enjoyed our marriage. I try to recall some angry moments and I can say it comes hard. So far, baby, so good.

When we got back to the States, we went to Moline, Illinois, to see Louis' parents. Well, Louis said, "You go over to the store with me." His father had a music store. "No," I said, "you go see your father." Louis and his father had been apart for two years. I said, "Let me tell you something. You go, because you're not the kind of person that could maintain something within yourself that long, these hard feelings. And this is your father. Now, when you see your father he will see me." Louis said, "How can he see you if you don't go with me?" And I said, "Because when you walk in and you're not unhappy, you look marvelous, your balance is all there, and you look better than before, then with his wisdom he will know me. A man or a woman is reflected in the person they live with and live around. If we were living it up, or being characters, and you walked in so he could see his son all dissipated, he'd say, 'I know what kind of life they lead.' "

So Louis went to the music store; I did not go. He said they looked at each other and cried. He came back after about a couple of hours and he said, "Dad says come over to the house." Now he had to see me.

I'll never forget when I stepped across the doorsill. There was warmth and understanding from that moment. He said, "I am Mr. Bellson." I said, "I'm Pearl." That's all. He knew that Louis' wish was acceptance of his wife, with all the great love, that family love, and that's the way it was.

10

My new life with Louis was wonderful for me. He was a goodness to hold on to, and from the time of our marriage I also had two other persons who meant very much to me: Don and Peetney Redman. Her real name is Gladys. Good friendships are difficult for performers to find, and many performers, like me, have learned to appreciate sometimes the loneliness and independence that go with the business. Usually, though, there is someone who really is close. Since Don's death particularly, Peetney has been someone who means this type of companionship to me.

Don used to come to the Pearl Theatre in Philadelphia in the old days, and I would go to see his show. At that time all the big bands, Jimmie Lunceford, Don, Louis (wonderful Pops) Armstrong, all played the Pearl Theatre. I didn't know Don then, but I knew who he was: one of the better of the bandleaders. Tops.

At one time, at the Fay Theatre, Fortieth and Market, I was in the chorus line on the bill with Don's band. He knew my brother Bill, and would speak to me, which was

126

a thrill. But my first real association with him came when he arranged some numbers during the war for Cootie Williams' band. We were working at the Savoy Ballroom, and Don brought up a thing called "Get Up, Mule." He ended up arranging most of the things I did with the band.

I still hadn't met his wife at this time. When Louie and I got married, I think the closeness with Don and Peetney began. Coral Records asked me to do some work and I asked for Don to do the arrangements. After the session, Lou invited him to come down to the house for dinner. This was when I met Peetney. Peetney told me later she was wondering what kind of person she was going to meet, because Don had spoken of me. You know how women are, meeting each other. They want to know how they're going to be. And she said she walked in, naturally thinking that since I was in the theatre she had to be primped all up. I had dinner ready, an old dress on, and no shoes. I opened the door and said, "Hello, honey, come right on in." It just struck her right. Then and there, she said, "This is a *person*." And that was the beginning of our friendship.

Then it got to be a regular thing. Either they were down with us or we were at their place. In general we saw them about four or five times a week, going to Madison Square Garden and other places. We became very close.

In 1954, when I went into *House of Flowers,* Don didn't have the band, but he was doing a lot of arranging. The producer met Don and asked him to consider being a policeman in the play. He was always known as "the little giant," because he was just a bit taller than Peetney, who's under five feet. He was nice and round, and warm like a butterball. Don had never been in a play, but he took that job and that brought an even closer relationship. It was a change of pace for both of us vaudeville folk.

Possibly the best thing to do when a project has ended is to take a trip. So, when *House of Flowers* closed after about five months, we decided to take a rest. Don, Peetney, Mr. Reilly (my dog), Louis and I piled in the car and headed west. Our destination was Vegas or California. We traveled at a snail's pace. We cooked outdoors but didn't sleep out. I'm not quite that much of an outdoor girl.

Off we started at 10 A.M., four musketeers on vacation. Our first goal was to get to Chicago in a hurry, because we figured the wide open spaces didn't start until we were past the Windy City. Stopping at every Howard Johnson's along the way didn't help our speed, so by midnight we had only reached Harrisburg, around 160 miles from New York. Next day we vowed we'd make it for sure. Where do you think we reached? Bucyrus, Ohio—so we did a little better than the day before. When we finally got to Chicago, all of our budget money was eaten up or spent for souvenirs. We had to cash checks and begin again.

It was a lovely trip, with Peet gathering wood and me as "chef." Lou and Don had the pots and pans to do. Oh, how they grumbled! When we arrived at Kingman, Arizona, at the edge of town there was a fork in the road. One side went to Vegas, the other to California. We chose California.

I looked like a blown-up balloon by then, I was so fat. In fact, we all should have hid in some local forest—we'd lived it up, and we looked like real lovable bums.

When we got to Victorville, I asked at the Texaco station whether there was a place called Murray's Dude Ranch around Apple Valley. I remembered it from USO days. Well, everyone knew and loved Mr. Murray, so the man gave us directions and off we went. When we finished following those directions we were sitting on top of a hill. There was one family up there. We began all over. It was hot and we were hungry. We were about to give up and return to what we called civilization when the place loomed into sight. There under a tree sat this wonderful man, Mr. Murray, that we were to grow to love as a friend and to cry for at his ending.

Our intentions were to stay one day—and that became three, during which time Louis and I decided that California was for us. We drove around looking for just a small spot to buy. Mr. Murray, ready to retire, spoke of perhaps giving up thirty-five of his forty acres. He would keep five, as he said, "to die on." Louis and I had no intention of going into such a deal. Whatever would we do with that much space? It sounded ridiculous to us. There were two musicians staying there, the only boarders. They kept telling us the old man wanted us to have the place. Finally, we spoke to "Boss" (everyone called Mr. Murray that), and told him that not only was it too much space, but it was also a case of spending that kind of money.

He said, "I'm not interested in the money now. I don't have to worry about that because I've owned the ranch outright for so long. It's just keeping the place clean and right that bothers me. Just give me something to let me know you'll be back, something to bind the agreement."

Lou and I had no other argument. That spot represented peace and contentment, so we okayed the deal. The next day Mr. Murray walked up the slope to the huge swimming pool and stood there gazing into nothingness, and he wept. He didn't know Lou and I saw him. Then he came to the cottage and said, "I'm ready," and off we went to the bank. I think even the people in there wept a bit when the paper was signed. Mr. Murray was an institution.

We left and went back to New York to get ready to head for the desert. We named the ranch the Lazy B, and there were questions as to why. Aha! Get this reasoning: I told Louie people would pass by and look at this huge ranch and say to themselves, "There are actors in there, leading a glamorous life. I wonder what those 'lazy B's' [dirty word] are doing there." Also, B is for beaver, and let me enlighten you: we worked like beavers from sunup to sundown. That's where guests and relatives and I sometimes clashed; they would come to visit Lou and me, and right away would want to sit Louis and me down in our own home and treat us like stars or something. When will they realize that Mama taught me to keep a clean house years ago, and I've not forgotten it, show business or not. I enjoy doing my own work. Secondly, how could we get relief from our theatrical work if we can't release that tension by wandering around our place getting joy? Thank heavens I've learned to be a good guest in other people's homes, learned it from the ones who came into ours and tried to take over. Folks who go to visit someone and must have something to do should go home and do it.

On the ranch we planted trees (Arizona cypress, the big

boys), raked, cooked for a large group, chased a few snakes (and I'm scared of them), pulled weeds, got tumbleweed from around all those acres. All I can tell you is that New York was never like that. There were no lights outdoors on the place when we started. That desert is dark. As far as a telephone was concerned, we had to go to the highway and use a public one. It would have cost a fortune to run a line back there. I was happy because I hate the telephone. They are misused instruments. Don't you love the people who wake you and ask, "What do you know?" I always answer, "Plenty, but I'm not going to tell you this early."

Talk about a hick, that's me. Once I planted flowers all around the thirty-five acres. You can imagine how many times I bent my aching back and, would you believe it, they were all poisonous? A gorgeous desert plant, but if put in the mouth, the harm was done. So, with children around, it wasn't the thing. I had to pull them all up—in 110 degrees yet.

When we moved to the ranch, the main buildings and all the cottages were in terrible condition. Often I have to laugh at the thought of someone dropping in on these theatrical folks looking for "big-shot living" and instead seeing us on this place. We even used iron beds and cots. We took the bitter with the sweet. At least we knew what our dream was for the land.

Once when we had to go East and stopped over at Mama's in Philadelphia, we went up to Germantown to see my sister Eura. She wasn't home, but my nephew Billy, his wife Roz (from England), and their three children, Debra, Felix, and Billy, were there. He explained that things weren't going well with him. His work and a couple of other issues were getting him down, and he wanted to leave Philadelphia. We said, "We are not able to pay a tremendous salary, but you're welcome to come out to the ranch and act as foreman." They were elated, soon got on the Super Chief and came on out.

Now it was a group of city folk on the ranch for sure. There was no kitchen in the big house, but there was a huge kitchen-dining room that had been used when the ranch was working, so we all had room to eat together. I cooked three big meals a day, and we really went to town building our dream. Louis and I had a small house built and made it a lovely home. Billy and Roz redecorated their house. We ordered a telephone and outside lights, and the ranch became a city.

It was a pleasure to see folks drive by and look at what we had achieved. We lived there for nine years, and one day will probably live there again. So much is there—the earth where food can be planted, the lovely sunsets, the air, and all that space to wander away and get with God.

God gives us all signposts to guide ourselves by. Sometimes we get confused and wander off on the side streets from the main highway, but if we can only remember from which direction we started, we can find our way once more to the main highway and go on to our true destination. How do we know our true destination? Look around at all the falseness when you reach a dead end and you will know. Many times because of our confusion we cannot or will not face up to the fact that we are on the wrong road. This, of course, lies within ourselves. If we ask God for the answer we will surely get it. He speaks only truth—and He means for us to go only one way. Face up—wake up and head for the main highway. Walk straight. Should you wander off, keep in mind where you came from. These are the thoughts Louis and I have carried all these years away from the place, and they have sustained us. We have opened our hearts, and can live with ourselves every day, knowing the earth awaits us again.

I want to write more about Peetney. She and I were never as much alike as our husbands. She is careful and conservative, and I have such a great drive, and am probably more aggressive. To me, it seemed she used to wish and worry too much. Heaven knows what she thought of the nutty things I used to do. We are quite a pair. I look like the mama (and perhaps tried too often to be one—out of love).

In those days, I'd say, "Come on, let's do this or that," and she'd say, "I've got to write a letter." Next day, "Did you write your letter?" "No, I'll do it tomorrow," and that would be the day we had tickets for an early show. So we'd have an argument over whether she'd be ready or not. Actually, she didn't even bother to argue with me. She just paid me no attention. But the bug would be the next day, over the decision about what to wear and whether her hair needed washing or not, all at the last minute. As great as her taste is in clothes, she'd always ask how she looked and was it right? I'd tell her it was great, and, lo, she'd change it. What the hell. It was her right. But I wondered why I had to waste time saying something that was going to be ignored anyhow. When we had these scenes, Don and Louie thought we were maniacs but, bless them, were too clever to tell us. They knew we were like two fighting sisters.

At Christmastime and before birthdays, Peet used to say, "I don't know what to give." It was a ritual with her and led to the same answer every time: "I love you and Don. All we want is your friendship. If you want to give something, I use and need what every woman does: perfume, soap, etc., etc." But she'd never follow through on that. Once recently (and I'm smiling, Peet, as I write this), she asked me what I wanted for my birthday. I said, "Dernit, I want a swimming cap." She said, "Ah, come on, you don't want a swim cap," and I responded, "Yes, I do," because I had bought a wild bathing suit in Canada and my dogs had eaten up my cap. "I need one. When you come to see me next time I'm looking for my present." I didn't get it. She wanted to give me something better, something I could use—but didn't need.

Once in Cleveland, I saw a little bank in the gift shop at the motel. I purchased it and gave it to Angie (sax player and dear person). It had a hand which came out and snatched the money. Boy, how we laughed every time that happened! When I went to my dressing room that night, I noticed the bank on the table and thought Angie had brought it back because it knocked me out so, but it wasn't true. Peet had seen the true joy that simple thing gave me and had gone downstairs and purchased the last one they had. I hugged her for understanding and giving me simplicity and joy.

The thing I want more than anything, and strive hard for, is to stay the same on and off the stage. Many people are so different onstage. Then there are those who never get off. People ask Louie and my friends, "Is she like that at home?" Mentally and physically there is no other side to me. The audience can get it in a song, and at home with my loved ones, it's the same feeling. I only want to give and receive one thing: love.

Rarely do I become close with females. We're difficult persons. Peetney and I have found so much in common because our lovers were so beautiful that some had to rub off on us. She always had a wonderful quality that I admired: she never meddled in her husband's business. So many wives of musicians, especially writers and arrangers, are forever making friends with people to peddle their husbands' wares. Not Peetney. She knew Don was a master, and his work could and would stand on its own merits. It's so good that though Don has left us, spiritually he's brought Peet and me such a great understanding of life. He not only left the world his music, he left us the true meaning of friendship, and Louie keeps us even. He and Don are two people from another world. It is something to draw on people who have taught us even more truth than we realized we could have. When Don passed we knew that in truth we had lost something in common: she her darling husband, who adored her, and I one of the nicest things God molded out of the clay. Don had a great influence on my life. What this man contributed to music would fill a book. I can't say he's gone or that it is death. He went to rest, and I know he's enjoying himself and bringing music to all around him.

Lately, Peet and I have been reading a lot together. I sent her the books *Life and Teaching of the Masters of the Far East* and *Letters of the Scattered Brotherhood*. We have learned how to accept pain. Don and Peet were married thirty-three years. Peetney had always lived for Don. But, as I said before, we all discovered that God will not let us lose our own lives. Now we spend many times together, she, Louie and I, always with peace. This rebirth has brought me closer to knowing God. I've watched Peet, and that little lady is strong and beautiful. The one thing humans don't like to recognize, unfortunately, is God. Would you believe it? The thing they need most, and already have, they deny. Well, Peet, we have now tied all the silly knots and no longer are "Testers of Each Other's Personalities" but real people.

Louis and I were on the train traveling from the ranch in Apple Valley to New York City when Mr. Bellson passed away. My father was in the hospital at the time and I was coming East to see him and my brother, who was also very sick, before going to New York where Louis and I were going to work.

We had about a twenty-minute stop there in Kansas City, and someone knocked on the door and said, "Telegram." I was sewing (making a tapestry pocketbook) and I had all this thread in my lap, and Louis had the table up writing an arrangement. Neither of us cared to move at the moment. I said, "Oh, could you slip it under the door?" The man said, "No." I asked, "Can you tell me through the door?" The conductor said, "No, it's for Mr. Bellson." So I got up and opened the door. He said, "We'll hold the train for a few minutes." Louis got off and I waited awhile. Soon I put the sewing down and went out in the corridor, looking out the window for Louis to come back.

I saw him walking back past the window, and as he came up the corridor of the train, coming back to the room, he just said, "We just lost Dad," and started working on his music again. I'm sure he was in shock. It seems Dad was sitting on the floor, nailing a cabinet, laughing, and he fell over. He hadn't been sick as far as anyone knew. Mr. Bellson was a man of great strength and silence (inner and outer), and he wouldn't have said anything anyhow.

So we had to get off in Chicago and go down to Moline. Not long before we left home, Mr. Murray, who sold us the ranch, had died and Mr. Keyes, who had been the chef there with Mr. Murray for eighteen or twenty years when this ranch was famous, was making biscuits when he heard of Mr. Murray's death. Mr. Murray had become very dear to us all. So when Mr. Keyes heard the news he just kept making these biscuits.

Then the day that they were burying Mr. Murray, I had the phone call about my father and brother being very ill, and when we were leaving to go see about them, I said to Mr. Keyes, "No matter what happens I'll just keep on making those biscuits."

So all of this came back to me as we were going into Moline. I wanted to keep well balanced, because someone would have to be the anchor for many saddened children. There were eight of them and it was a great grief; they dearly loved their dad. We call Louie's mother Peewee. She does not allow anyone to cook or clean for her, but she was so shaken this time it didn't matter. I ended up doing the cooking; it kept me busy, thank God. I sent for dozens of cans of frozen biscuits, and did what I'd promised Mr. Keyes before leaving home.

I always had a good relationship with Peewee. When all the discussion came up about our marriage, the reporters here in America must have asked her what she thought of it. The answer she gave was the most wonderful thing a woman could say. They probably asked, "How do you feel about your son marrying a girl of another race?" And Peewee said, "That is my son and whom he loves, I love." And this is the way Peewee and I have lived with each other.

At the funeral I had four on one side and four at the other; it was like my arms were long enough to stretch. That day of the funeral, it was as if Mr. Bellson had actually spoken to me and said, "Take care of it." I felt that way and tried. We miss you, Dad, and I want you to believe the arms are still stretched around all of them.

Those we love and lose are usually human. But now I have to tell you about Mr. Reilly. It took him awhile to get used to Louis because he was with me a year before I met Louis and during that year he was king. In fact, this was my only companion—a boxer dog. At the Beverly Hills Country Club in Newport, Kentucky, after the opening-night show, one of the bosses had come backstage and said, "You opened pretty good. What would you like to have?

When you're finished we're going to give you a present."
I said, "I want a dog." He said, "You're kidding, what do
you *really* want?" I said, "No, I'm not kidding; I want a
dog, a boxer." During the week he'd come back from time
to time and say, "I'm looking around." Well, it turned out
that his missus knew quite a bit about dogs of good breed.

The club was way up on a hill; it was a very prominent
place. One night, as I came around to the stage door, there
he stood waving his arms and saying, "You better hurry up,
girl, if you want to see this thing, because I'm going to
get him out of here." He was smiling and kidding me.
There with all the chorus girls and musicians was a big
brown clothes basket, and everybody was gathered around.
In there sat this little fellow, nine weeks old.

We decided to keep him backstage and started thinking
of names we might give him. He really lived the life. He
had all the girls, and he was in all the dressing rooms.

They had a piano backstage, and one night rehearsing a
song I came across a number John Rox had shown me
years before called "I Want to Live the Life of Reilly."
Looking at this music I thought, "Gee, I'll run over this
tune between shows." One of the verses went:

> *I want to live the life of Reilly,*
> *For whom I feel most highly.*
> *I want to live the life of Reilly,*
> *Mr. Reilly and me.*

I thought, "That's going to be the name of this dog."
He got his christening right there.

When Louis and I got married, Mr. Reilly would just
sit in the middle of the floor and look at us, because here
was another person in that life where he had been the
prominent one. He loved Louis, but he watched him.

Everyplace we went, people knew Reilly. He got choice
bones in the nightclubs, and he ate with every actor between shows. He was loved.

In 1954 I had a robbery while I was in *House of Flowers,* and of course Mr. Reilly was not there; he was at the
theatre with me. When we got home and discovered the

robbery the police photographers were anxious to take pictures of this tough-looking watchdog. Mr. Reilly jumped up on the bed, and they got a marvelous picture of him looking down into the empty drawers and things, as if to ask, "What happened here while I was gone?"

Much later, in 1960, I had another robbery, while I was in Vegas. This time Mr. Reilly was asleep in the living room. He was quite capable of protecting the suite, but the thief knew his name and all the affection that went with it. We had just had a wedding there in the house for a trumpet player, Guido, who was marrying one of my little show girls, "Miss Toronto," named Darlene. One of the fellows who cleaned the rugs for the party had been playing with Reilly that day, and all the time planning this theft, I guess. He came in the back window, which leads to the bedroom. Mr. Reilly probably roused from his nap in the living room, heard, "Hi, Mr. Reilly," and thought it was a friend. So Reilly wasn't such a great watchdog—not the right nature, which may be why I loved him so.

When we moved to the ranch in Apple Valley in 1955, I just kept getting dogs and dogs, what with thirty-five acres. They were welcome. This city girl in the country was a bit lost and afraid on that dark desert, so I was especially glad they were there. The more the merrier. But Mr. Reilly was still king.

Reilly started staying home when we traveled, and I guess he missed the road. About this time, I got a big Weimaraner, and he used to sit up and just lick Mr. Reilly's face. He accepted the fact that Reilly was boss. His name was Sandro. Now, Sandro never left the ranch. Then once I took him to Vegas when my friend Jean and I were going to see her husband, Nick, who was playing with Lou's band in the lounge at the Flamingo. We were driving late in the evening, and we thought he'd look mighty protective on that back seat—and he did!

Ordinarily it would have been Reilly going along, but Sandro looked so fierce and Reilly was a little older now, so we took Sandro. Louis lived on the second floor of the Colonial House, and when we arrived everybody stared at this strange-looking tall gray dog with gray eyes. Up the stairs he bounded, a beautiful thing about two years old. Later he was ready to have an outing, but there were those stairs to come down. Living on the desert in a ranch house, he wasn't used to them. So he was cringing at the top of the stairs, and Louis had to pick him up and drag him down. It was embarrassing because people were watching, and we're dragging this monster down so he could go. I guess he thought he was on top of the Eiffel Tower or something and wouldn't come down.

After that trip Sandro thought he was boss. Mr. Reilly was about eight by this time and hated fighting, but Sandro's jealousy became so great he would attack him often. Well, we got rid of Sandro.

I still had about seven big dogs. Then a boxer and the Weimaraner had mixed and all nine pups were black as night. I'm not an artist, but I know gray and brown don't make black. But there they were. Soon we were shipping big dogs away and giving them to people passing by. Oh, they were wonderful animals.

We took a trip East and were gone a couple of months. When I got back and drove into the yard, there was Mr. Reilly enclosed in a pen, poorly fed and dirty. No one had been coming out to give him love and warmth. He looked old, and I could see something was wrong. He had gotten very, very fat.

I was furious. I said to Mr. Keyes, "He's so fat!" "Oh, he just put on a little weight," Mr. Keyes said. Later, I was in our big kitchen, ironing. It was a little chilly, so I had a fire going in the fireplace, and Mr. Reilly was standing there watching me. I heard a sound, turned, and this dog had keeled over. When he fell like that, it really frightened me and I rushed to pick him up. A nephew of mine—Eura's child, who was visiting at the time—said, "Try to be calm, Aunt Dick. I was going to tell you that I think Reilly's got heart trouble or water in his lungs."

Louis took him to the vet's for a checkup. After we brought him home he was all right for quite a few weeks. Then Mr. Reilly started having dizzy spells again and falling. One night we took him back to the vet's and left him. The next morning, about a quarter to ten, the doctor called while I was having some coffee. He said, "You'd better come up because I don't think he's going to make it."

It was about three or four miles to the vet's office in the town of Victorville. Well, in fifteen minutes we were there. The vet's mother and he were standing there, talking about Reilly's condition. I was wondering at this point when he was going to take me to see him. Finally, I asked, "Listen, can't I see him just a minute?" And he said, "Oh, he's gone." I just got up, walked out the door, leaned against the car, and the tears came. I didn't speak, but the tears kept coming down.

The vet's mother was crying. The vet was crying. Yes, even the doctor loved Mr. Reilly that much. We got in the car and drove back home, weeping unashamed.

11

―◦◦◦―

Back in 1955, soon after we got the ranch, we came back to New York and became parents. One Wednesday night in July, while we were living on Bank Street in New York, Louis and I received a phone call concerning a child. We were asked if we wanted to take him into our home and lives—a baby boy, an infant in need of love. It was such an abrupt way to hand over a human life that at first we hardly believed it. What could we say? Our hearts were so filled that we should be so blessed. Louis was working with Duke at the time on a date in town, and I was working but had Sunday off. We told the people we'd be there. They told us to come as soon as possible. Frankly, at that time I had no desire to see the real parents, but we were getting the baby directly from them. I couldn't get into my mind how a person could do this.

Sunday we took off for this town to get our fine son. There he was, this lovely baby boy nineteen months old, in just a diaper—no undershirt, no shoes—big wondering eyes staring at Louis and me. He might have been wondering if these two folks would leave him stranded later in this big world. Well, Son, we're still around.

Louis named him Tony, and it's all right for Tony to read this, because he has known about his adoption since he was seven. When he got his wish—a sister, who was adopted, too—we told him. He knows that he is loved, and that he must never think harshly of anyone concerning any of this. After all, by accepting us he's had the pleasure of making two people happy.

Anyway, that day we got him, boy, we drove home fast with our precious gift, and all night long we watched this guy lying between us, changing towels because we had no diapers yet. What we found him in was his complete wardrobe. Early the next morning we called and ordered a crib and a potty chair. We told the store *definitely* a potty chair, if not the crib. My son and I grabbed a cab, me in a light summer dress and he in his washed-out diaper (dried quickly by the oven), and headed for the store for wardrobe buying. I stopped at a small store on Twenty-third Street and Eighth Avenue and bought him a pair of rompers to wear on our way to more fancy buying. Back in the cab and up to the children's floor of one of the finest stores in town. Folks were looking at me a little strangely. Shoes, socks, underwear, pajamas, the works. And panties, no diapers. I believe in training early, and to my mind this guy was behind time already. Dressed to kill, we returned home to Papa Louis, who was happy to see the crib *and* that all-important chair. Mr. Reilly, who by now was Louis' baby, had to take a back seat. He didn't mind the baby, but he got so snappy for a while that we thought he did. We discovered he did mind having his title given away. He was resenting someone else being called "baby." Louis gave Tony a nickname, "Toto," and from then on Mr. Reilly was all for him. When Reilly died, Toto missed him as much as the rest of us.

At that time Lou traveled with Tommy Dorsey, and I was often on the road, too. I always took Toto, the crib, the chair, and a record player. By all means music went along. We have raised our children on music and love. They've always been left to go to sleep with music, and when they were put on the floor to play I'd just turn the music on to soothe them. I never had screaming children, yet I have been strict. Soon there were uncles and aunties springing up all over—real ones and make-believe ones. Of course Don and Peetney were the first make-believe ones for Tony.

Our boy went everyplace, and I must say that traveling has paid off in many ways. We also got him books and more books. He's an avid reader at fifteen, and I hope he remains so. My world has always been greatly enriched by reading.

Tony is very artistic. Louis had a set of drums for him as soon as he could wiggle his fingers. He'd bang away. He understands drums, but at present he's an alto player in the school band, and a good one. At four he could draw as well as some twelve-year-olds, and he's forever designing something. I think Toto is going to be an inventor, designer, or something similar. But who knows what way the mind of a child will go? Whatever it is, Son, please do it well.

When he used to cry, Louis would play on the snare drum and that little rascal would stop. After we moved to Apple Valley and he started to school, he was no longer a showman. A funny thing used to happen whenever we returned from a tour. Toto would go into his room and bring out the drum and play it in a frantic way. For a while it seemed strange, but we decided that it was his way of showing his joy at our return. He played like a person possessed. Tony is highly sensitive and he rebels easily, but Mama has a firm enough hand to control that. He loves lots of loving. Someday he is going to be a fine man.

Though Tony had a lot of playmates on the ranch, when he went into the house at night he was lonely. He expressed a desire to have a sister. Well, several years after we got Toto, I did a film for an adoption agency and was surprised at the terrible difficulty of getting children placed in homes. Little did I realize that nice human beings with love in their hearts could be so choosy about giving a child a home. They looked at these tots as if they were something on display. Color, race, religion, all that was so important.

What about these homeless tykes who didn't even know they were to make an appearance in this wold? I thought about asking Louis for baby number two. He was overcome at the mention of a female, so I asked the people at the agency and they said, "Fine." At the time they must have thought it was a whim of ours, because we didn't hear from them for two years. Tony kept putting in his request every now and then. We were in Vegas when the agency called me to do a turn for them. It was impossible because of previous commitments, but I reminded them of their promise to me of a daughter. Soon after, a nice lady came to see us and said, after looking around, that they had come up with a doll that was suited for us.

While I was playing the Cocoanut Grove in Los Angeles, the call came. The princess was ready. Tony had been prepared for his sister. (The agency staff always talk to the other child in the home to see his reaction to having another child in the home.) We left the hotel helter-skelter to pick her up, and it was as happy as the trip we had made for Toto. We sat in a little anteroom and waited nervously. In they came with this three-month-old baby, placed her in our arms, and left. She looked into our faces and started smiling, and has been smiling ever since. When all the papers had been signed, we headed for home with our second blessing. Everyone in the show looked the little mademoiselle over, and she looked them over with her beady black eyes. We gave her the name Dee Dee (after Louis' sister) and Jean for a middle name (after a dear friend). I call her Sister. Females seem to develop faster than males. She walked and talked at eight months, and hasn't shut up since. She has a fantastic I.Q., a nine-year-old intelligence when she was four. Louis and I want our darlings to know we love them very much, and we cannot give them as much as they have given us.

While speaking of my children, it's a good time to pass along some of my thinking on the way children are being raised today. What do you accomplish when you don't let children think out things for themselves? I see mothers who tell children to tie their shoes, and before the child can bend down she beats him to the job, then screams,

"When will you learn to fasten your shoes?" I say, "Mother, when will you exercise enough patience for him to learn?" Why not thoroughly show the child once and let him go from there? Children are never as stupid as they can sometimes act.

One of the wonderful things about them is the way children answer any "why" question with the single word "because." You have to be awfully clever to get around that famous answer. I've chastised my children for that, and I was absolutely wrong. That is their answer: "Because." (But "because" can go on forever.) I've asked my son and daughter often, "Why were you late getting ready for school?" Answer: "Because my shoes weren't done." Sometimes to keep from going nuts I would decide to play the game of Because. So I would ask, "Why weren't the shoes done?" "Well," they'll say, "there was no polish." Question from Mama: "Why was there no polish?" I would go through the entire thing until they ran completely out of answers and stood looking at the sky. I would say, "Now I've heard the *excuses* and I want the *reason*." And so we started to learn. Then I'd say something like, "The reason was that you did not open your mouth to say the polish was gone. Now go to the store and get some."

My nephew T. Tony came to Washington to visit the Shoreham while I was working there. He hadn't been in the pool five minutes before a big wrestling match commenced with Exie, a stringbean friend of twelve, and my son. T. Tony was five foot nine and fourteen years old. He had Exie around his neck like a fur piece. Though they were only playing, it became a bit too rough. I got up from the table and bellowed (and I can bellow!) at the three boys. I knew without looking that every woman there had been watching me with my group. People watch theatrical folks and their children to see if we let them get away with crazy things. How wrong they are. Nobody could know the pitfalls better than we do. Some mothers call their children and they don't even move. I don't let mine get too far. With just my hands I can give the message to my children. Three movements work: "Come here," "Sit down," and "Stay." It's rather embarrassing for them, with their playmates watching and listening, but all of us that were properly raised went through the same thing. I remember how it is when you've been a big shot down the street, and now Mom deflates your ego. The other children are watching, and when you make that walk to Mom, it's *got* to be the longest walk of all.

The mothers I adore are those who visit you with an untrained child and constantly say, "Don't touch that again or I'll spank. Aunt Pearl won't let you come to visit again." This is usually after your nerves have cracked as you watch this darling child destroy your home. These mothers would be better off if they would stop reading those books and stop repeating that famous slogan "They're going through that stage." I say spoil them with love and discipline. Children adore it.

I've seen and taken care of what people call "monsters," and I've seen them transformed into darlings with proper training. Once more I repeat, this requires fewer cocktail parties, fewer long trips to the hairdresser for chitchat. It means not turning television on at seven in the morning and leaving it on all day. Oh! Some females are going to hate me for this, but, girls, I'm only trying to help you out of what you call your misery. It takes lots of unselfish attention, lots of it, to create a happy disciplined child.

Besides, kids are a joy to be with because they are wise. In Cleveland little Exie gave a good example when he was visiting us. I had come home about four or five o'clock from "The Mike Douglas Show." We sat down to eat, my children, Louis, Exie and I. Seemed like ages since I had had food and, boy, was I ready! At home before we eat, each one takes a turn saying grace at meals. I was in such a hurry to eat and I turned to Exie and said, "Exie, say grace." He said, "I don't know any grace." I said, "Well, say *something*. I want to eat. Say anything." He, by now, was really upset and answered, "What do I say?" I said, "Say 'God's good.' That's sufficient." The little fellow got mixed up and said, "God is sufficient," and I said, "That's good. Let's eat." I think that's the most wonderful thing, because reversing what I said to him, this child had said more.

The lack of discipline that I've been talking about has set confusion deeply into the minds of our youth. It's bringing disaster. Rebellion has become rampant. Where are we? What do we do about it? Let them rebel? No! I say tell them the truth, not half-truths, but "God-truths." Walk the path of life with them, show them we have no fear, and they in turn will adopt the same attitude. These are children groping, dear readers. They want a friend. They desire understanding. They crave love.

Oh yes, I hear the arguments now: they owe us something. Agreed. But we owe them something, too. God has entrusted these souls to our care. The least we can do is our best, every day, to put forth the effort for this cause. Remember, we want for them a future of peace and love with all humanity, and it can be accomplished only with our help. This is our next generation, so why not start to build now? Here and now is where the root of the trouble starts.

If we ever start to understand the simplicity of a child (the Bible says so), we'll enter into something beautiful. We must put their simplicity into our wisdom and our wisdom into their simplicity. Children, like a lot of adults, need somebody to *make* them do things. Man says, "I love God." One asks, "Does he love Godly?" There's a difference. It's the "how" that matters. If ever I fulfill my teaching desire, I'd like to do it with the method of Socrates. I would teach youngsters by asking them questions and having them think about their answers.

There's a connection between raising children and cooking. We haven't taken these dolls out and put them on the griddle of life, and let them cook a bit.

Living a full and rich life is like making pancakes. You put truth in a life and pour it out on the griddle with love. Then you should not keep lifting up the edges to see if it is all right. If the batter and griddle are prepared correctly, the bubbles will rise to the top, and you will know exactly when to turn it without ruining it.

My feelings about love come partly from experience of my own and probably go back all the way to Mama's influence when I was little. Mama never had it easy during those years, but somehow out of her came a certain sensitivity in all the children. Oh, through the years we kids had our spats and jealousies among ourselves all right, especially Bill and me, but underneath it all the great love is still there.

Even in our young life in Washington, D.C., Bill always had an influence on me. He had a wonderful knack for storytelling, a great sense of humor. And he was a wonderful artist. Not *was,* he *is.* He used to tell us stories, and I'll never forget the two names that he would use for the people in his stories. We were all just young children together, and yet this man had two characters going, like a serial, with something new about them every night. The lady was Miss Sabu, and Beau Didley was the fellow. But they didn't go in the same stories together. One night you might get Miss Sabu, and the other you'd get Beau Didley. They were just imaginary names that he had thought up. And this man would be as all wrapped up in these stories as we were.

At one point, in 1961 or 1962, Bill and I were working together. This was the most beautiful thing that could happen, for us to be together. In fact, my sisters could have joined us because we were all talented enough to work on the stage.

Bill had many, many good moments with the show, but he began to do some things to destroy himself in the business that he dearly loved. From the outside came the tidbits and the needling of other people, which always set the harm within. Sometimes he would scream, "You stole things from me, that's where you got it." And I say, "Never." He'll read this book and know—never. What I got God gave me.

We were fortunate as a family. God gave us all a great degree of talent. I learned from Bill, but I did not take from him. He had the wrong idea all the time. The reason I learned from him was because of my great admiration and respect for him, not only as a brother but as a great artist.

Well, while we were working together, my back was acting up and my legs were in a lot of pain. I would do the show anyway. Probably the music kept me walking, because without it I could hardly put one foot in front of the other. And by the time the curtain would close, it would be like my legs were paralyzed and I would pass out. Coming out of this one night, I heard my brother yelling. He had gone to pieces; it was the first time I ever collapsed in his presence and it scared him badly. They didn't move me because they didn't know what had happened. I was out cold, and they wanted a doctor to see me right there.

Anyway, when I was coming out of this thing, I could hear Bill screaming, "Do something, do something!" He was going to pieces because no one was doing anything. Well, the owner was there and he was trying to tell him, "Bill, we've sent for a doctor." But Bill was just like a madman he was so worried about me.

Now, Bill was a dancer and I wanted him to straighten out his life. I wanted God to say, "Walk, Bill Bailey, on those feet I gave you. I will leave your sister the voice and the hands." I wanted Bill to dance. And I said to him then, "If God didn't want you to dance, he would have taken away the use of your feet. Instead mine have slowed down a bit—he let me have your pain so it would become visible to you and help you understand yourself."

Recently, I got a beautiful letter from him, which shows you, dear reader—and you, dear brother—the influence this powerful man must have had on me. What could you steal from a man like this, who gave himself so freely?

Dear Sister,

There is nothing more to be said in written words to glorify anyone in this world—nothing to top these words of praise heaped upon you and the cast of Hello, Dolly! They have written, so unanimously and descriptively, rich and rewarding expressions of love for you and the gift of talent that God has endowed you with. Such miraculous enthusiasm is amazing. This overwhelming spellbound love the public of all classes has bestowed upon you cannot go to one's head, for there's no head big enough to hold it or store it.

It can only humble one and fill him or her with humility.

We who are children of God know that all praises belong to God. The little portions of it that He lets us share are just tokens of His love—He lets us taste its soulfulness.

So we praise God from whom all blessings flow.

Now, rise and shine, and give God the Glory—Glory—Rise, shine, but give God the Glory.

Love,
Willie

In Washington one night in 1949, someone told me my father was in town. Papa traveled, so no one kept up with him. I knew he had been preaching in South Carolina, but didn't know they had switched him back to Washington. They gave me an address in the S.W. section and I went. There was Papa (good gracious) with children like stairsteps, ranging in age from two to nine. He was in two or three rooms with all of them and an oil burner for heat.

Jim, my husband then, and I bought a house in a lovely neighborhood and fixed it up for Papa. (Jim was in real estate, remember.) Papa and his wife said it would help if we could take at least one of the children, since the wife was expecting again. So the one called Doll came to live with us, and we really dressed her like a doll. Instead of a half sister, I began to think of her as my own child; but every other day I'd take her home and take the other children something so they wouldn't feel bad. I didn't want Doll to forget her brothers and sisters. As much as they seemed to enjoy our having her, they also seemed to resent her appearance. The mother looked at her strangely, too. Doll had learned so much that they would just stand in the living room and look at each other. This hurt me. I knew eventually she would grow too far away from her mother. I could see it was a mistake, so we returned her. It broke our hearts, but at least she had a start, and recently I talked with her about this. Every time I'd see the family, Doll would look at me in the strangest way, so I astounded her by saying, "Doll, for all these years you've looked at me with love and hate, and I know why."

She said, "How do you know?"

I told her, "I have a gift for that. You have wanted to know all these years why I, whom you thought loved you, gave you all the pretty things [she admitted she remembered the places and things], then took them away and made it all ugly again."

It was so true she could only stare at me. Finally, she said, "Why did you?"

I told her there were other people concerned, and I couldn't hurt them, and she was not to blame anyone.

Ofttimes a family is really all so close, whether you realize it or not. I felt it when Henry, my seventeen-year-old brother, passed. I'd only seen him a few times. Still, when he died I wrote a letter, my way of expressing grief. Please read this, dear hearts.

TO MY BROTHER HENRY

Life stopped for you, little Henry, January 5, 1964 You are the first to go, sweet youth. God plucked you from among the aged and started the cycle to move It was swift, dear brother, and though I didn't look on your face I was with you. I shall sing from the heart to you only tonight. "Poor Butterfly" will be yours tonight, and some will cry, not even knowing you. Papa never lost a child, and now at eighty he must experience this. Carrie sounded sad and alone when I spoke with her (a mother's insides). You sister Doll was bewildered—and I am unable to understand what Death is. May I add now, perhaps it Beauty.

Papa will be talked of for many years by the medica men who took care of him, I suppose, as almost a miracle He was a powerful force. He never had a tooth pulled they just dropped out, and he went on from there. The firs time he was ill—at seventy-nine—he came home on a train alone from South Carolina or maybe Georgia, wherever he had been preaching. He made it and they took him to the hospital. He had had a temperature of 105 for two or three days, which is fantastic.

They sent word to Louis and me that he was passing; we should come. Of course, he was in there screaming for them to let him out because there was nothing wrong with him. Four times he had pneumonia, in addition to TB, at seventy-nine. Very prominent chest surgeons would call us in from California. His chest had black spots, and at one time they called it "galloping consumption."

Each time he was ill he told the doctors, "I don't have anything." One time they sent him to a sanitarium. Papa said, "Get me off the floor with these old people, because there's nothing wrong with me." He wanted me to sign him out. What a decision, knowing the medical report! Then the doctor walked in and said, "He can sign himself out because he doesn't have anything. It's gone." And nobody has ever explained where the tuberculosis went.

This man walked to the theatre from the southeast to the northwest section in Washington. Papa didn't believe in going to the theatre, so I was amazed to see him in the wings. They took him out front. He had never seen a show. Afterward, I said, "Papa, you're going to California with me." At first he said, "No, I can't go," but the next day he changed his mind.

"Do you want to fly?" I asked him. "Great!" he said. He'd never been in an airplane in his life. So I told him, "Blanche Shavers, Charlie Shavers' wife, will pick you up and bring you to the airport." Then we were out at the airport waiting—no Papa. He was sitting in the yard to wait for his trip to California (Blanche was late). I had them put him in a cab, and luckily the plane didn't leave on time, so we made it.

Louis and Papa ate all the way from Washington to California and Papa entertained all the stewardesses with his great stories. The only thing that amazed him about the airplane was how they could fix eggs twenty thousand feet up in the air.

Peewee, Louis' mother, was there visiting us, too. One day I got them both these comfortable chairs and sat them down under a big pear tree while my friend Jean Di Maio and I were digging holes for rosebushes. Peewee was talking about her children, and problems and all. Now, Papa was thoroughly enjoying this desert sun, just living it up in his comfortable chair. He loved all the service he was getting. He was saying to her, "Be happy, woman, be happy. Look at us: we're so lucky. There's Louis. You have a wonderful son, and look at my wonderful daughter. And here we are underneath a wonderful pear tree, and we're really living."

Jean and I were listening to this conversation as we dug away. Peewee kept going on and on with the complaints. She said in her broken English (remember, she was native Italian), "Oh, me have to complain, me just wish I were dead." Now, it was about 112 degrees, and Papa kept trying to fan away this conversation. He raised up his head and said, "Look how good God is to you. There's the hole, so why don't you just get in it? How lucky you are—there's the dirt right on the side! Pull it in after you and shut up." And of course Jean and I collapsed with laughter.

Two days after we got there, he was helping plant these big Arizona cypress trees. My father was a hod carrier in addition to being a reverend, and maybe because of his Indian heritage he had done some magnificent things in stone, clay, and pottery. Now on the ranch he was boss of everything, putting these great big trees down and helping dig holes.

At one point Papa was trying to make us take him to Los Angeles to the House of Prayer meetings. I said to him, "Papa, I brought you here to rest, and the people in the church can understand it. It's a hundred miles, it's hot, and afterward all those people would be coming down here and there would be no peace." We were walking over to the big kitchen where we used to eat.

He said, "When do you go to church, baby?"

"Every day," I told him.

He said, "Every day? I've been here a week and I haven't seen you go to church. Where is the church that you go to every day? You never go outside this fence."

I said, "Papa, you see this ground? This is my floor. Do you see the mountains? They are my walls. And the sky, that is the ceiling of my church."

He stopped and said, "Where did you get all this wisdom so young?"

"I guess I got it from the same Man you've been talking of for some time: God," I said.

He never again asked me about church, because he understood how I felt. Every day that one can step out on this earth and feel the ground under his feet, he has attended some sort of church. It's the man who is walking on the ground and doesn't know its value and strength who needs the stone building to convince him.

Papa went back East and, at over eighty, scratched a toe closing a suitcase. He would allow no one to touch it, and next thing we knew gangrene set in and they said they'd have to amputate. It had spread, so most of the leg had to be cut off. When Louis and I walked into the hospital room, he was sitting there with the stump of one leg crossed over the other, and he was rubbing the stump with his back to the door. I said, "Papa," and he looked up, straining. He couldn't tell who it was because almost all the voices in the family are the same. I said, "It's Dick and Louis." He had no idea that we had come all the way from California. He looked at Louis and said, "Oh, Louis," and he let out a little sob, and then it was gone. That's all I've ever seen of that sort of emotion from my father. He was a man of great humor, dry, and a philosopher.

The doctor came in and said, "Mr. Bailey, your daughter wants you to go home with her. I think it would be good. You would be out on the level ground with the wheelchair, and she says she could push you around and everything. We'll think about it as soon as you get on your feet."

And Papa says, "What feet, man. I only got one foot."

Doc said, "You realize that sometime you'll lose the other leg."

And Papa said, "I will never let you take the other one."

But in November of 1966, when Papa was once again back in Washington, the other leg was taken. When it happened, I wrote a letter to him. Not a letter to send, but one from my heart to his. Papa was a wise man, and a powerhouse, even at eighty-four. He was a wonderful father. I started off with a little poem, "Where Are My Wings?" His feet were his wings. Papa was always on the go.

I was sitting in the bathtub in Indianapolis, Indiana, and this came to me. I started to write what I thought were his thoughts:

WHERE ARE YOUR WINGS?
(A LETTER TO PAPA)

"Where are my wings?" you ask, dear bird,
Without them I can't fly.
And so you sat day after day,
Saying that you would die.

(This was a rare statement because he never, never said anything was over. But suddenly we heard he had lost his will to live.)

But if your nest is feathered well
And you have been a man
You'll think you'll grieve, you'll smile,
You'll pray,
But die you never can.
For Death has no wings to take away,
No power to give the call.
Only God has the inside line—
Dear Papa, He's got it all.
Give even from your feathered nest,
There is much wisdom left.

Then I was saying, "Papa, while you're sitting there, don't give up."

Ask God to give you faith enough to see yourself
whole and new. Only the material flesh has been
nibbled upon by cause and error, but God has taken
away nothing. He has given you the strength and

knowledge and extreme wisdom to deliver more to mankind. I really hope to be able to gather in more knowledge from my father's feet. All the time you've spent speaking, living and praying have endowed you with a great strength. Pull on it, dear father, with all thy might. And even if it breaks, you will not have lost. Because of the truth that you never stopped trying. That is sometimes what I think God will always want us to do. It may even be the true religion—trying from day to day. Each day does bring new things, and so, religiously, we must work each day for even more truth. Papa, I hope to see you soon, in good spirits, good health, and your beautiful frame of mind. Hang on to truth, and it will make you free— of everything.

I did not know that Papa had been admitted again to the hospital for the time that would be his last, until I called Mama one night in November. You would think someone would have let us know as soon as he went in. Then, after sending cards and not knowing the details, I did a strange thing. I sent yellow chrysanthemums. No reason except that they were large and I suppose I thought he could see them better. His eyes were that bad by then.

On Louis' and my anniversary, November 19th, my manager, Stan Irwin (an angel), sent us, of all things, a large array of flowering plants: yellow chrysanthemums, yellow daisies, and birds of paradise. They were beautiful and seemed to bring a special light into the house, so instead of putting them into the living room I kept them in the kitchen, where I stay most of the time. I called Stan and told him how they seemed to be brighter than any I'd seen, and after ten days the blooms were as alive as on the first day. That Monday, I called the hospital very early and the doctor said, "I think you'd better come. It doesn't look good." It was touch and go.

My mother-in-law was dropping in again (from Illinois) and I went down to the station to meet her. The next day I was to do a television show, which I called off. I was getting my thoughts together about leaving for D.C.

that day or the next. After picking up Peewee, I did a rare thing, which was to sit down during the day and start to crochet. (I usually work my fanny off all day and don't believe in dillydallying in the day.)

Suddenly I got up and went into the yard. There was a tree in front where I had planted flowers I'd gotten from my own stay in the hospital. Mr. Keyes at the ranch had told me years before that if you take a slice of white potato and put it in the ground as you plant, it will help root anything. So I got a potato, cut it (not counting the slices), went into the kitchen, picked out some of Stan's flowers (without counting), then went out and dug holes (without counting). The reason I'm stressing the not counting is the way it turned out. I went out to plant the flowers. I had the feeling I was burying Papa. So I put the first plant down and all the emotions came forth and a voice spoke, "Weep not, my daughter, you have done well," and the tears went away. When I finished my planting there were six flowers, six potatoes, and six holes. Also, there were six of us, in Papa's first family. At six that very evening Virgie called to say that Papa was worse, so I told her I'd meet them all in Washington the next day.

My readers, to tell you of the things that happened in Washington might make you think of me as a mystic or something, but you will do me a favor if you let some of these things sink into your heart. Every man has his time to face this. One must go one step beyond to get to the basic truths, to know there is God. Whatever, whoever, or wherever, there is something man cannot deny, though he tries hard.

When we arrived at the hospital from the airport, Papa was breathing so hard I thought of the expression "the death rattle." I heard this sound and saw my papa lying there, so thin, so gone. There were a couple of the children there looking hopeless, but I felt wonderful inside that Papa had waited. You see, I had this beautiful feeling that Papa had waited for me and the flowers. I kept repeating in his ear, "Papa, we are here with you—Louis, the yellow flowers, and Dick." He had not moved since Sunday. I did this on and off for at least two hours, but those closed eyes, and the gasping breath were my only answer.

Everyone left the room for a while, and I started all over again pleading for Papa to please let me know he knew I had come, just to let me love him a bit longer. It was shocking—yet I didn't get frightened—when the sheet moved and this hand came across the chest and touched mine. I never moved my hand, but his and mine met and the hand locked. I showed the others our hands. I wasn't holding his; Papa's was locked on mine. Papa let me know. We were always so very close to each other. He had an understanding of life which I needed, and he put it into that hand squeezing mine. It was the one tie I had waited for all my life to put the polish on my soul.

This has not been easy to write, because, as I write, that day of his passing is only two weeks past. We looked alike, we philosophized together, and Papa never called that I didn't answer, thank God. Mama told me that I had been a good daughter, and that makes me feel good, folks. Tonight there is no sadness in my heart. I had always thought that death would be frightening and ugly, though through my own illness in 1965, I had lost that fear for myself. It was seeing it for others that had me puzzled. He looked so unreal. They had amputated more. There was nothing left, just this tiny creature lying there wanting to go, but holding on until he had given all. Some said they couldn't bear to look. Well, all I can tell them now is you missed the most beautiful thing in your life, watching a powerful force like Papa go peacefully to God.

The doctors had a hard time telling me. They sent for me at one point and were going to speak of Papa's end, but I got them absorbed in listening to talk about the book I was writing, and we saved ourselves. It must be so hard for men of medicine to have to deliver these sad moments. Doc, with all your medical knowledge, you had to sit back and watch helplessly. You were so young, and though you had done your work well it was hard for you to take that leaving. Both of us were holding on to something that day—you with all your medical power and me with my love power. God took his scissors, cut the rope, and we both fell back. Nobody won.

I was kneeling by the bed after Papa was washed. I knew that Papa was gone then, though they told me he lasted till the morning. In our talk we had, the docs were helping me over the hump. I remember that second morning I arrived at the hospital. The docs looked at me strangely. They thought I had gone home. Now I realized that Papa had gone and they were not ready to tell me. At that time perhaps it would have been too much, but little did they, or even I, for that matter, know how much I'd seen of Life and Death, gazing into those eyes of Papa's. He saw me and I saw in his eyes "I am free and able to walk straight"—complete release from all fear forever.

Later, as you read of my own experience in the hospital, you will realize what I'm saying here. I can only give you an example by telling something that happened in Berkeley, California, after my own illness. A man was telling me of his son who had been ill and was still a bit confused by it, so I wrote a note and told him to give it to the boy: "Death reached out its hand, I did not respond, and he went away." I had written to this boy what had happened to me, telling him what I had overcome. Papa went with Death because he was ready to "see" more, and I must remain to "learn" more. With you always, Papa, in our school of love.

12

---◆---

In 1956 I had an engagement in London, and Louis
and I wanted to take a trip before I opened. We had been to
Rome once before for four days. That time we had flown
over the Alps (so I could say I had flown over the Alps).
Italy was so wonderful. It knocked me out so much in
just those four days that we wanted to go back. Four
days was just too quick.

So we decided to take a trip to Italy for ten days before
my London thing. We took thirteen pieces of luggage.
Now, I was going to really rag out, to be just out of this
world, you know. I was taking all the fur coats and everything, because I was going to really dress for these Romans.

We had been playing the Flamingo and I remember it
was the first time anyone had stayed there seven weeks. Mr.
Parvin, the owner, was so wonderful. He gave us a bonus
to really enjoy our trip. So when we left I had everything
just so; I was going to be dressed to kill.

We got into Rome in the morning, and in Rome they
close everything around one o'clock and they don't open
again until four. They really take three hours to eat. We

decided, naturally, to go out on the street and shop, then go home and take a little nap, then go back again to do some more shopping. And what did we do? You know. We went to sleep and when we woke up it was like two in the morning and everybody was through, it was over. Now we sat there and we ordered some food and someone brought it to us. We sat around till about breakfast time, just talking and everything, looking at our souvenirs. We decided we might as well go out after breakfast and do some shopping.

So we went wandering around the city again. While we were out we rented a little car and a fellow named Felicci. He took us touring the countryside in the little car, and, remember, I've got those thirteen pieces of luggage on top. We headed for Genoa and went through Florence.

And on that trip we also went through a place called Montefiascone. There they make the finest wine in Italy. They don't sell it outside that village. Ordinarily I don't care for wines, except one I've had which is called Liebfraumilch, but I even mix that with soda. We stopped in a little inn, and the old lady inside said to Louis, "Taste this." She had a real big bottle of wine, and she wanted me to taste it, too. She wasn't going to give up. She was thinking if I don't drink the wine I have to be out of my mind. I thought it was going to be sweet, maybe like a soda pop.

So I had a sip of it. I wet my lips to keep from offending this old lady, and when I licked my lips, I had never tasted anything like that. It was so good, just unbelievable. So I got the whole bottle of it, which they sold us for sixty cents, and took it with me.

Then everywhere we went they would bring up the luggage and I would bring up this bottle of wine in a bag and set it on the dresser. The waiters and everyone would come in and say, "Ah, Montefiascone," when they saw the wine. They would go crazy, because this is how famous this wine is. Just a little sip of it would last with the taste of it on your tongue all day.

After we explored Genoa, we continued on to Portofino. There's a saying that if you ever go to Portofino you must go back. They do not build new things in Portofino. You can repair, but you can't build new things in this particular village. It is as it was, and that's the way they want it to remain. It must be one of the most beautiful spots in the world. It's right on the Mediterranean, which is a blue I've never seen before, a blue you could only see once in a lifetime.

We stayed there in this hotel in Portofino for three or four days, and one day we got on a little boat and went around the bend to a place like a cave where an old monastery had been. At one point the waves part and you think you see something down in the water—and there is. A huge statue of Christ, and his arms are raised up. The fishermen lift it up every so often and clean it and everything. San Fruttuoso is the name of the place. And when you get off the boat there on the beach, you see just this empty monastery, an old building. It must be hundreds of years old.

Well, after touring around, Felicci, this boy who was our guide, drove us on back to Rome. We gave him a tip, like we would do at home, and I think it was much more than he had ever made or expected to get. And he cried, just like a baby. He had become very dear to us. Wherever we stopped, he would want to wait outside in the car. We would say, "No, we're all going to eat now." And then he would come inside, but he was going to get another table because that's the way they do. He was the chauffeur and he was going to sit someplace else. Well, we wanted him to sit with us, and he just couldn't get over that—the fact that we ate together. And when we wanted a room, he was going to get a room in another hotel. We said no, he was going to stay in the same place. And he couldn't get over that, either. It was just wonderful to see this boy. I'll never forget him, a great person. I still write to Felicci all the time. He has a beautiful little baby now.

When we got back to Rome, that wonderful city, we went to the opera. I thought, you know, if you go to Rome, you've got to go to an opera, and I had never been to the opera before. Well, I wanted a cigarette during intermission. I didn't know what they were talking about anyhow, this singing, you know, the screaming. And some man had turned around and started to talk to Louis about the music and all. So I walked out by myself to the lobby to have a cigarette.

I was standing there, and my head was down while I was lighting the cigarette. Well, suddenly I had the feeling that somebody was watching me, and I was never so right in my life! I was on one side of the lobby and there wasn't a soul there but me, but when I looked across the lobby the whole side was filled with people standing there looking at me. They were all saying *"Ah,"* you know, *"Bella, bella,"* and different things. And they were all smiling at me. They seemed to sense the stranger, and one thing that was attracting them a lot was that I had on a cerulean mink coat, a blue-gray mink, full length. I don't think they were familiar with it over there at the time. You know, we were beginning to have fabulous mink coats over here, all kinds of wild colors. And suddenly here was this *grande dame* at the opera with this long gray fur, whatever it was. They hadn't even figured, I don't think, that it was mink, but they knew it was an elegant coat.

When we'd first come in, Louis had handed the tickets to the ticket taker and the man couldn't even take the tickets he was so shook up. He didn't have any idea Louis was Italian, you know, so he was saying, *"Ah, la bella signora"* and all like that. These people really were saying these things, even out on the street and in places when we were shopping during the day.

And I remember whenever we were in a store and they would pull out something for us to look at, if a little bug or a spider came out they wouldn't kill it. It seemed like the Italian people feel that the spider is a lucky omen. Especially if he's crawling to you. I feel the same way about a spider. I'm not superstitious, but I've never seen a spider in my life that something fantastically wonderful hasn't happened to me. Years ago I used to catch them. They say if you catch them and keep them, you know, it's lucky. And at that time I did have the superstitions going for me.

I remember these people would say to me. *"Ah, faccia simpatica."* Louis explained it to me; they were saying

I had a sympathetic face. Everywhere we went, they would turn in the streets and just point at my face. *"Faccia simpatica!"*

So at night, you know, when we were going anyplace, like when we went to the opera and all of that, I had a little mascara on and everything. Well, I still got the same thing, *faccia simpatica*. So I said to Louis, "You know, the *hell* with this sympathetic face. Now, I want to be called *gorgeous.*" Becuse, really, I had on my best finery and I was still just a sympathetic face.

We also went to Alfredo's; he was world famous for his fettucine. Years ago Mary Pickford and Douglas Fairbanks had been there and Alfredo served them with a gold spoon. You still get a gold spoon there, a replica, I guess, of what he made up for them. The old man died recently, but when he was alive, he really could sing, so he'd sing to the customers and then he'd go in and get the food and bring it out. Everywhere the mandolins were going. *Arrivederci* was everyplace. It was really very, very wonderful.

In so many people on that beautiful trip I saw the same warmth that Louis has. I could see that same sensitivity that has meant so much to me in Louis through the years.

Louis and I have always enjoyed some of the same dreams, and in 1959 we decided to try to live one of the dreams we shared. Vaudeville has always meant so much to me because I started that way. It's sad to watch the theatres in America (with the exception of Radio City and maybe a few more) ignore live entertainment. To think that the children of America have been denied this rare privilege. Oh, sure, the nightclubs are around, but they're not the same. Where are the chorus girls, the first and second acts, and so on down the line? All folks see now is a "concert tour"—one big act or seventeen screaming small acts in some monstrous auditorium, poorly lit, with terrible acoustics. The performer just isn't presented correctly. This brought about my idea to revive vaudeville, and we hoped other performers would follow. We wanted to bring in big bands and introduce new acts to the public. Ten of us crossing the country, playing the closed theatres, could have started the ball rolling. Of course, it would mean a lot of work for all.

The agents argued that it was useless and couldn't be done. They were proved right, because no one else took up the baton and ran the race with patience. But I figured we came into this business to entertain the public, and folks are everyplace. We could do a good thing for the man who couldn't afford the prices of some of the high-class places. These people put us where we are, after all.

Well, with this theory, off I went with Louis and our troupe of—get this!—sixty-two people. Now, I admit that was too many, but every time some aspiring youngster came along and wanted to try, we hired him. We made one big mistake—we mixed amateurs with pros. The young ones deserve a chance, but only after their "dues" have been paid. Taking the money that we had made and saved from working in Vegas, we headed East. The whole mob went first-class all the way. The drawback was that the bookings had already been made for me alone, so the owners got a complete revue for the same price. I paid for it, because some of these same owners later tried to drop my solo price. They said I must have worked for peanuts after paying off that crew. The fact is that I didn't work for peanuts, I worked for nothing. I didn't make a dime, but I still had my dream. Many of the kids had never left the Coast and they were seeing the country for the first time. I scrubbed a few bathrooms in places that hadn't been opened for years. We looked at empty houses and prayed. There were a lot of people who thought we were fools. But out of it came a bit of hope. I still get cards and letters from some of the people in the show who remember. And people throughout the country still mention seeing the shows. It took Lou and me awhile to pay off the loss, but God was with us and we survived that.

Regardless of what anyone believes or thinks, someday I'm going to try it again, because I believe in getting to the people who can't get to us. In King Arthur's day the jester went around and played, not knowing how he was going to make out. He did it for love, and picked up bread on the way. With all the expenses performers have today, we might as well do the same thing. We don't come out that far ahead. I say, have a ball—it's only money, and chances are that some false friend or close annoying relative will get it anyway.

I believe that a person must go ahead and do some of those things that are important. Most of the time you first have to make an opportunity.

In 1964, I got a chance to do something else I'd wanted to do for many years. I'd heard so much about people in institutions. Are they the ones who are mentally unbalanced, or are some of us? Some of those outside belong inside, and some of those inside belong out, I suspect. In going back into their fantasy world, the mentally ill may find some truth. Some of us outside never know the truth at all.

It's not always easy to judge, though. My father told me a tale about a lady named Miss Ida in an institution in Georgia. He'd visit, talk to the patients, and pray with them. One day he went out there and Ida was horribly scratched up. She told him they had beat her, which upset him greatly. My father asked the person in charge, "What are you going to do about this? These people have mental problems. It's a shame to beat them." The executive said, "Well, let me tell you how Miss Ida really got the scratches. Do come outside." Miss Ida had gotten out of the building, taken bricks and broken every window on the ground floor. It had taken nine people to subdue her.

There's much humor in what these people do sometimes, and a sadness! Miss Ida had the smartness to know, "Someone will come along who will believe me."

While I was working a club in Pittsburgh, I met a lady and told her how I felt about people in this condition. She happened to be working at the hospital in the town, so invited me over. I began to wonder—how would I take it, and what would I do when I saw them?

I went on the condition that I not be asked to perform, because I wanted to listen and learn. Some of the patients had seen me on television a week before. They were playing cards, having their cigarettes, and telling me what happened on television last week.

Then we went to "maximum security." My escort was a lady official I called "the Hostess." She said, "This is Miss Bailey, Pearl Bailey, who's come to see you. Do you want to meet her?" You would have thought this was the dearest friend I had. She told another lady, "Let me tell you what Pearl and I are doing. We're going to dance." A woman looked up and said, "Oh, shut up, just shut up and sit down." I was amused because this was a typical female statement.

Sitting on the window sill was a girl about twenty-four years old. It seemed she had destroyed her baby, or thought so. She said, "You read the papers, don't you? You know about me?" I said, "You lost your child. Babies, very young, sometimes don't make it." The statement I made about the baby being so young just struck home. The baby *was* very young and she *had* tried to destroy it. She had only come into the hospital about two days before and I did remember reading about her.

The patients generally kept their heads down, but when they saw a hand, they would look up, smile, shake it, then go off into some weird conversation. One very elderly lady started stroking my hand, making guttural sounds. They say it was the closest she had come to speaking in ten years.

Then there was Mrs. Smith. She had her food tray and sat turned away from everyone. I said, "Hello." She just looked up and wouldn't speak. She didn't want to be bothered, so we left her completely alone.

After that visit, I decided not to leave town right away. I couldn't. Louis and I came back the next day with a big grocery box filled with chewing gum, candy, and little gifts. The girl on the window sill stayed on my mind, the one with the baby. A chocolate flower pot with a purple flower sticking out of it caught my eye as being just for her.

I had on my slacks, a big straw hat, and carried a pretty walking stick someone had given me just for fun. The Hostess really greeted me that day. I went around the bend, and there, lying on a bed, was the young girl, completely out of this world. I said, "I told you I would be back and I brought this. So now you must get up." She got up, laid her head on my shoulder, and stroked my hand.

Suddenly Madame Smith came in and the chocolate pot caught her eye. She said, "You're going to give it to *me*. You have no right to give that to her, because you're the same as I am. You should be bringing that to me."

I wouldn't give it to her. By now, I felt I knew how to talk with them and how to cope with them. I said, "Behave yourself, you don't feel well today, Mrs. Smith. It's warm and I don't feel like playing. You're not getting this." My hat went to one side—Mrs. Smith had reached up and snatched the butterfly from it.

Louis wandered into the room. She said, "Who is he?" I said, "He's my husband, Mrs. Smith." She said, "He's nothing, he's absolutely nothing. Throw him out." She would have nothing to do with him. She wanted this girl's flower pot, decided I didn't need my walking stick, and took that. I didn't mind her having the stick, but it was very heavy, gold encrusted on the top, and I thought, "Wow! What she could do with that stick!"

We gave everybody some candy and they were having a party when Mrs. Smith reappeared and hooked her hand in my bracelets and rings. "Take them off, you don't need them, you're no better than I am." I took them off and she put them all on. When we started to the recreation room, the nurses asked Mrs. Smith to give back the things.

Now Mrs. Smith was giving us nothing. She said, "You're not going out of here." Everybody was sweet-talking her. The nurses said, "You mustn't do that, Mrs. Smith." The situation didn't frighten me, but I knew she had to get handled by these nurses, and the ward might become disturbed. She said, "You and I are leaving together, because we're going to fly to see Lizzie." Number one, I don't care about flying; number two, I didn't know who Lizzie was. I said, "I'm not going to fly to see Lizzie today because I have to go to Washington, D.C. I can't go with you this time."

I was trying to get her to move a bit from the door so

that they could unbolt it and we could leave. But there was no moving this tiny lady.

She said, "Don't be slick, you just don't be slick."

"Let's talk over here," I said, "away from the door, and we'll discuss Lizzie."

She said, "We're going to discuss Lizzie right here, with me standing by the door."

The others were crowding around, saying, "Mrs. Smith, she's nice." They pleaded like little children, but in vain. Someone thought of another exit, so we acted like we were going to discuss something and went out the kitchen door. We went down to the recreation room, where there were lots of people, and sang and danced for at least an hour.

There was a handsome young man who wanted to do a solo, a fellow who was about to be released. The piano player didn't know the song, so he sang alone. He made a big circle, walking and singing "People—people who need people . . ." Tears were trickling down their faces as he sang.

All the time this activity was going on, at the end of the room I could see a mess of hair over a face. As we started to leave, this person came over to me and said, "Don't go." I pushed the hair to one side, and saw the face of a madonna. It was a girl about sixteen years old, one of the most beautiful faces I have ever seen.

I asked, "Why do you want me to stay? I've been here some time, singing. Everyone is happy and having a nice time, and you're the only one that didn't enjoy it. Now you ask me not to leave. Why?"

She said, "Because you have given me something."

"You only get what you give," I said.

She answered, "But suppose I give so much, when do I get it?"

I said, "When you're giving, that's when you get it."

The nurses seemed amazed the way these people were responding to Louis and me. Louis had played a little set of drums, about two pieces, and it was amazing. A little girl broke into hysterical tears. I held her in my arms. We all felt the "oneness of humanity."

They introduced a boy of fifteen. He walked right up and started talking about Einstein and things that you would expect to hear from a grown scientist. I said to the nurse, "I know what's wrong with him. He was brilliant and his parents probably sensed it and pushed him too hard. There was no playing, no boyhood."

Then there was another one, about fifteen and a half. He was one of several youngsters in with the older people. He was as cute as could be, a handsome boy, with such a twinkle in his eye. He kept edging by the door, and I knew what he was trying to do. He was going to go out the door with me when we left. They said he had gotten as far as the fire escape a week before and had built a little fire.

One lady was highly amusing. The gestures she made to explain herself were quite risqué. She must have been six foot one, had only one eye, and a flapper bob. She was very, very thin. I had a feeling of not wanting to go over to her, because although I had felt no fear with anyone, I felt strange about her, wondering whether to touch her or not. I had learned that if you touched one of them and they withdrew, you must walk away. They don't care to be disturbed. They have gone completely to their world of fantasy.

I spoke. She looked up in my face and broke up laughing. Hysterically. I said, "That's not fair for you to laugh at me." She said, "Honey, don't have a man, don't have a man. They are the worst things. All they want to do is —." She made a gesture of sexual relationship. Then she broke up again and that was it. We all had to laugh. It was contagious.

A nurse walked up just before we left and gave me my jewelry. I remember thinking that they must have given Mrs. Smith a shot or something. She said, "Oh no, she decided herself to give it back. She just said, 'It's not mine.' "

Driving down the turnpike, we stopped at the Howard Johnson's. I was looking for some change in my huge pocketbook and started pulling things out. There was a comb, some letters, and assorted other things, and on all of this property was written the name of Mrs. Smith. I don't know at what point the lady had dropped her things in my purse. I returned them all to the hospital. I imagine she had thought she was packing her bag to go see "Lizzie."

On another occasion, Louis and I had a similar experience at a hospital. Louis was going to play there for the patients, and they wanted me to sing some songs. But I was thinking how much feeling music can stir up in people. Louis would be playing notes, but I would be saying *words*. And suppose I sang a song that had words about love, words that would mean something strong to some of them. These words might penetrate and bring even more sadness.

As I was walking down the corridor of this hospital, a little old lady came out of her room and said she wanted to hear a song. I said at first, "No, I don't want to sing a song to you." But this charming little old lady, she put her head on my shoulder and I started to sing "The Old Rugged Cross." I got through a few words and saw her tears. I said, "You see, I told you. I shouldn't sing these songs for you." She just kept her head there, and the little tears kept coming, but I stopped singing the song.

Then we went into the maximum-security areas. Louis had visited there before. He had brought home, from one of the patients, a painting of a clown. He had wanted me to have a gift and Lou had told him I collected clowns. The painting didn't exactly frighten me, but the clown seemed strangely real. I said, "Louis, this is more than a painting. It's wonderful, but it's not just a painting. This person, whoever did it, painted himself." The eyes were that alive. The face was chalky, but it wasn't the chalk like it would be in a painting of a clown. It was the color a person's face might become.

We went into maximum security, Louis and I, and I've never seen such works of art as those people were creating. Suddenly this fellow walked in the door, the man who had painted my clown. There *was* the clown. It was true, he had painted himself.

It was warm. They were outdoors, standing—some looking at the grass for hours. It was strange to see humanity standing by the side of the road of life, waiting. We are considered "sane," yet we, too, stand waiting beside the road of life. We are almost the same as these people, because some of us don't know what we're waiting for.

Are we in better shape? At least *they* have found some world into which they can go and find moments of happiness. If we, in our sanity, could find even more moments like this and retain our senses, wouldn't we be better people? We have lost some of the values that these people in their fantasy world retain. You see one caressing a child or a doll, giving it warmth and love. Some of us need to reach back into our childhood, not to hold, not to possess anything, but to remember and cherish some of the beauty of our lives.

13

"Tired" came out of 1944 and 1945; it was the first record that I made, and it's a song that will live with me always. A wonderful team, Doris Fisher and Allan Roberts, used to watch me work back at the Blue Angel and then they wrote the song for me. They also wrote "Fifteen Years" and "That's Good Enough for Me," which were the first records I made with Columbia Records.

I used the song "Tired" as a warm-up; it's a theme song. But to say I'm tired, that would be an absolute lie. I do think that now I know more about what the words mean than I did twenty years ago, because I've lived a little of life and I have been tired, mentally and physically. But if I have a problem, it's the opposite of tiredness. Like Peetney would say when I used to get after her about being slow to act, "You don't understand, Pearl; you have such fantastic drive and force," and you *know* that's a nature of mine.

But that song had a great impact. So many people meet me and their opening line (it makes me laugh) is, "Honey, aren't you tired?" And it gave some people the idea that

I was a Stepin Fetchit character. It so stuck with me that at times it's almost turned me against the song, and I have refused to sing it. Now every song writer wanted to give me something about sitting down on the floor or dragging along, and people began to accept me as a tired, slow-moving person. After a while, instead of getting peeved about it, I began to be very amused, because I know in me I have this terrific drive. My husband will tell you, in housework or anything that I really step out to do, there are going to be very few that can keep up with that drive. I mean, I can start my day with very little sleep, but once I get into something, I go strong.

Going to work one night in Vegas, I stepped on glass. It went right through my shoe. I called the doctor, did two shows, and hobbled home. Doc told me I had to have a tetanus shot by noon the next day, at least. But, dear hearts, I was there long before that. By nine the following morning, Pearlie Mae was in bad pain. Big Tony, my brother-in-law, said, "I'll go along," but misery didn't need company that day and I went by myself to get the shot. The next day Tony had to pick me up in his arms and carry me like a baby, whether I wanted it or not. I got a pair of crutches and a soft pillow to rest my foot on for nine or ten days. The hotel called and called to see if I could make my show, but I was unable to put on shoes. True, I've worked before with some aching situations; however, this was something that might have truly endangered my career.

On the bill with me were the Maldonado Dancers, and that marvelous man of whom I'd heard but had never seen except in movies, Mr. Harry Richman. We were booked for two weeks, wonderful. Harry was a treat to watch. I think he'd been ill long before this date and had not been working, but now he was all aglow like a boy, working again. I used to watch this man without his knowing. His dressing-room door would be open, and the room was immaculate. He'd go home between shows, return, and go up to the stage (no one was in the show room between shows) to play songs and compose while nobody was there. Harry wrote "Walking My Baby Back Home." He'd tell me about all the greats of the business—Nora Bayes and people of that time. My, how I was learning! His shirts were so pretty, and I told him I admired them, so he sent Louis some in Chicago. This man has so much class it rubbed off on everything he does. When I got hurt, Harry was kind enough to come over every day. It was so cute to see this dapper man coming to cheer me up with a bouquet of flowers, and it was sad in a way, too. You must imagine this man who had been such a big star now almost completely ignored, not by the public, but by people whom he had helped and loved. He didn't seem to mind, but, dear Lord, I'm sure it stung a bit inside. Still, he walked with beauty in his soul for his fellow man.

Leaving Vegas, I went into Los Angeles, spoke with a doctor who looked at my foot. Next stop: Cedars of Lebanon Hospital. That was the first time I ever spent an entire week in a good quiet spot.

In early December 1964, while I was working in Palm Springs, something occurred that started the final growth of Pearlie Mae. I was about to come of age, to learn my limitations. After this job I was to go to Puerto Rico on February 22nd, but I never made it. Deep down something kept saying, "You will not go." I wanted to work there badly, having never been there, so this feeling seemed strange, not kosher.

Not too long before this, Peetney, who had been visiting and gone to Hawaii, had noticed a crazy feeling I was having. Many times, laughing, I'd get a sharp pain, which I guess changed the expression on my face. Peet would ask, "What's wrong?" and I'd answer, "I feel a little something here," and I'd point to the chest. Peet insisted I have it looked at, but, having a hard head, I didn't go to a doctor. The pains weren't frequent, but, boy, when they hit, they shook me.

One day around then, Louis and I were sitting in the living room and my inner communication center told me, "The phone will ring." It did. Eddie Fisher was at the Riviera Hotel in Vegas and had to leave ten days early to do a special for the President. Could I fill in? Since Lou was going to Japan, I okayed it. Home after Palm Springs, a short rest, then Vegas, more rest, and Puerto Rico. That was my plan.

Lou left and Angie (my sax player) stayed around with the children and me until our Riviera date. When I'm about to leave home, whether the person with the children cooks well or not, I cook a lot of food and put it in the freezer. That's what I was doing when this thing suddenly hit me. Standing at the stove, I "died." Angelo was sitting at the kitchen table watching me cook, not knowing I was "gone."

Since we had only recently moved to Northridge, we didn't have a family doctor, so I called the babies' doctor, who recommended a man. I dialed—no answer. I had another call to make, to Nick Di Maio, Jean's husband, to set up the time for leaving the next day for Vegas.

He asked, "Is that you, Pearl?"

I said, "No, I don't have it. It's all gone."

"You sound funny, is that you?"

I assured him it was. This man had now known me for seven years, and yet he couldn't place my voice. Later he told me I'd sounded like I was under water.

I hung up and I called the dentist to tell him I couldn't keep an appointment. He said, "Are you all right, Pearlie Mae?"

"Yeah."

"You don't sound like yourself."

I said, "Come on, Doc, you know my voice. To tell you the truth, I was trying to call a doctor. I feel like everything's gone."

He said, "What do you mean 'gone'?"

"I just don't have it."

"Well, why don't you try the man who came when you had the mumps?"

I took the number, called and asked if I could come right over to see the doctor. The nurse said, "He's seen his last patient and he's going to dinner." But, you know, somehow you've got to believe in something, because she turned from the phone and then said, "Just a minute." He came on. He said he was going to dinner.

Finally he said, "Well, can you be here in twenty minutes?"

"Oh no, I live out in the valley," and he was in Beverly Hills.

So he said, "Well, I . . . uh . . . I'm going home."

"Yeah, but you've got to see me."

"Lady, but I haven't had anything to eat all day and I want my dinner."

So I said, "I'll tell you what. Why don't you go out, have your dinner and come back, and by that time I'll have time to get there."

He said, "Oh no." Well, it was about quarter of six. He said, "Could you be here by seven-thirty?"

"Yep." I just put on black slacks, and at seven-thirty I rolled in there. Angie drove me down. For three hours the Doc and I sat there (Angie fell asleep in the reception room) and all we talked about was books and life, just talking. And the last half hour, he said, "Let's look at you."

Now, I had never asked anybody how my heart sounded, because it had never mattered. I had heard people say that if you ever heard your heartbeat it would frighten you. But I said to this man, "Let me hear what it sounds like, Doc."

Doc said, "Let me see how your ears are." So he put the ends in my ears and I listened. I don't know how a heart's supposed to sound, the rhythm of a heart, but I thought it should be like a musical beat, in time. He took the ear things out and asked, "What would you say?"

I said, "Off tempo."

He said, "Off tempo." He just looked at me, like a verification. "Lady, you have no energy, no reserve energy. You have nothing to draw from. The only thing you have [and he did know something about my life from the conversation we'd just had] is spiritual strength, and you're going to have to draw from it."

He still was not saying there was anything wrong with me. He just asked me how much I smoked and that sort of thing. Then he said, "Now you're going to Vegas for ten days, and when you come back, you are going to go away and take a little trip."

I said, "Oh, my husband can't take a trip with me right now."

"I didn't say your husband, I said you. Now, I don't

care where you go. You can go to Acapulco or Palm Springs, just go."

"Yeah, well what's my husband going to think? I can't just go to my husband and say, 'Honey, I'm going away for a couple of days without you . . .' "

He said, "If he doesn't understand, you tell him to come to see me. Go ahead, relax and enjoy it. After these ten days, come back in and get an electrocardiogram." I decided that if I did what he said maybe I could go to Puerto Rico, after all. He was leaning on one side of the doorway, and I was leaning on the other side. And he said to me, "Now you relax and you rest. Get a lot of rest. Because if you don't [now this was the most serious he had been with me], you are going to be very sick."

And I said to him, "You mean very, *very* sick?"

He said, "I mean very, very, *very* sick."

So I left.

I went to Vegas and I did ten days at the Riviera—one of the best engagements I ever had. The dressing room was lovely, and everything was just right. You know that habit I have of lying on the floor between shows wherever I can find a rug? Well, they had a lovely one. And Jeanie Di Maio was with me. She's a very warm, wonderful person, so there was a lot of love around me.

Louis came back from Japan about the second day, and I told him what the doctor said. And he said, "I think that's wonderful. That would be good for you." Understanding Louis.

I had a record by Tony Bennett that I used to play in the dressing room: "Who Can I Turn To?" I knew there was only one to turn to—God. I knew what the Doc said, but I didn't know what he meant. I had never thought about my heart. Now it was definitely something that caused concern. But I enjoyed my work, the show was going well, and I felt beautiful inside—ethereal.

Two days before I closed, Debbie Reynolds, who opened next, caught the show. Next night the poor thing had a strep throat, couldn't open, and I filled in a couple of days for her.

Then we were going back to L.A. on Route 6, a threelaner. I never liked that road; it always seemed so danger-ous. There was a big crowd up the road. I looked out the window and asked a lady selling tangerines what was wrong. She said, "Somebody had an accident up there." For some unknown reason I jumped out of the car, ran up the road, and the next thing I knew I was a nurse. One girl was sitting in a small car, just staring. Later on they found that her pelvis had been broken. She was in shock, I sup-pose. I didn't touch her, but smiled, and she smiled. I kept telling her, "God will take care of you." There was a man by the curb, head mashed. Then there were an elderly lady and a man in a big car. The blood was pouring out the back of the lady's head. Bystanders had a sweater, holding it to the hole. I kept talking to her at the window. She was asking if her husband was all right. First she was say-ing, "Go away, go away," because she didn't know what she was talking about.

Her husband said, "The lady is just talking to you, honey." It was incredible. The whole back seat and the floor were bloody. I've never seen so much blood in my life.

A little old man came up and said, "Move over."

I said, "No, I'm talking to this lady."

I was going from one car to another, so he asked, "Are you a doctor?"

I said, "No, but are you?"

"Yes."

Then I ran and got Angie and had him go into the restaurant right there and tell them to send all the table-cloths out. Everybody was standing on the side of the road looking; nobody was moving. Luckily, we had a big first-aid kit in the car. (This darling old doc didn't have a bag, probably retired.) Here was Pearl (Nurse Edith Cavell), all her bandages and all . . .

My appointment Monday was five o'clock for Doc and six o'clock for the dentist. Louis was out. Count Basie called and said his drummer was ill and asked Louis to fill in for a record date. I figured I'd have dinner ready so Louis, Angie, and the children could eat. Then the wave came again. Not pain, just that wave of "It's gone, there is nothing else." So I put the tops on everything cooking, and turned the stove down, and said to Angie, "It's all done. Everything's just simmering." I went back and put on my slacks, sweater, and kerchief.

He looked at me and said, "Gee, you look wonderful. You don't look sick."

I said, "I'll probably go to the hospital, but everything is fine here."

He said, "Do you want me to drive you down?"

I said, "No, I'll be all right."

The nurse gave me an electrocardiogram. I had to walk on some little stairs and then lie down. After she looked at it, she dashed out of the room, came back with Doc, who put this little white pill under my tongue. I didn't know what they were doing, but I heard him tell her to let me lie there a moment and then take another. I was happy to be lying down. I was so exhausted. After the second one, the nurse said, "You can put your clothes on." I was putting on my sweater when Doc walked into the room with his coat on.

He asked, "Where the hell do you think you're going?"

"You know, Doc, I told you I'm going over to the dentist."

He said, "Lady, you're going to the hospital, what do you think of that?"

"Great." I had spent about a week in a hospital in my whole life, that's all. I followed him. I didn't even call home. I just stepped over and said, "Let me make one call."

I called Jean and said, "I'm going to the hospital. Later, Alligator."

I was so in a fog. I tramped right behind Doc, got in his car, and off we went, having a ball all the way. I can remember most of the ride and the admitting clerk asking my name and everything. They put me in a wheelchair and rolled me right up to Intensive Care. Later they told me my heart had almost stopped twice. Doc told me I'd been near death. What does it mean, "near death"?

Louis called home to say, "Tell Pearl the record session

went overtime and I'll be late," and heard I was in the hospital.

After they moved me out of that section and upstairs, I was in the hospital for twenty-one days, from the first of February, 1965.

There was a doctor who came into the room every day, and one day he let his profession down by a silly incident. I'm sharp, sometimes too sharp. When I've been pushed I have many times been brutally frank. But I attack only when attacked. This man said cruel things, unethical things. The respect one can have for people of such a great profession should not be disturbed by evil acts, but I guess it's just that doctors, too, are human. Though we are all a part of the world, sometimes we become too much *in* it. When we can dig deep into our souls, we realize that all men have not grown up. All of us do not accept the fact that our work and life should be wholly devoted to God. There is no other debt to pay.

One day, talking to Marie Bryant, who'd lost her beloved husband, John, I said, "Humans want to turn loose and fully trust in God. They say, 'I've got my hand in God's,' but they seldom entrust both hands. One hand is in his, but how about the other? It's holding on to the material things without which we think we cannot survive. We are thinking always how would friends and family like us without these material things. We think we'd swing around in nothingness like puppets with a string broken. The reason we don't want to turn completely loose is the fear of the fall. What about the glory of the rise? Once both hands are up, we'll feel secure and safe. Oh, we'll swing around in the air a bit, but as the breeze of truth passes our faces, we will be conscious of all that has passed before and what will come."

Marie said, "Sheba, I'll go you one better and say we're only held up by His hands," and I said, "Can I go you one better? We're only held by a *breath*."

Mama didn't come to see me right away. I remember sitting there one Saturday night and there was a feeling, and it was starting to build inside. But I had learned to kind of throw it off, the feelings like this, but, still, it was like I was feeling sorry for myself because nobody had come, especially Mama. And that's the main one, Mama, the main artery.

When she did come in to see me, she said, "Oh, you look wonderful, Pearlie. You don't look like you've been sick." Inside I was lashing back: "Yeah, Mama, but I have, and no one came." But I held back and I controlled it. So we watched the ball game and we left it alone.

Mama wanted to pay for her breakfast. I said, "Oh, don't give me that bit," you know. She said, "I don't want to impose." I said, "My God, there's no imposition." Really, I knew the imposition had been that no one came. And, anyway, there is no price of a breakfast that could pay for feeling.

Well, about Wednesday, I was sitting there and suddenly the phone rang. It was a night call, collect, and it was Mama. She said, "I just wanted to call you and tell you how wonderful you looked. What a nice time I had." We talked a long time and I had to smile. I thought, "Isn't this something." I think Mama went home and thought about a few things. There isn't a lack of love there. I don't think she knew she was hitting me on the head. Mama, I think, has always been pretty warm and understanding.

This makes me think of a secret about me, and it has to do with Mama, too. It happened way back when I was on the coal circuit; we were working in Columbia, Pennsylvania. Well, at this time I was young, you know, and I did one of those things that you might do at that age. There was a carnival playing between Harrisburg and Reading. I saw this man with the needle there, and I couldn't think of anything to do but to have a tattoo. So I had my mother's name tattooed right on my leg. Well, I got to thinking about it after that, and I decided that Mama would find it maybe (remember, home was my base at this particular time), and in one way she wouldn't like me getting a tattoo!

So the next day I went back to the carnival and I had the man put a heart around this name. I thought that would help matters. I remember that needle didn't feel that good, but you're young and an entertainer, and you're at the carnival showing off, nothing hurts very much. Well, one day I was home in Philadelphia and I happened to be in the bathroom when my mother came in. And she saw this thing. She said, "What in the world is *that?*" And I couldn't think of another thing in the world to say but, "See how much I love you?" She said, "But you didn't have to put it in writing there, you know."

Well, I have got this thing well placed, oh boy. Right on my leg.

There was a lot of time to think in the hospital, and I hope I used it well. There are a few brains running around in this noodle. I thought about the doc, the young helper, who made the big scene. Maybe he had become despondent earlier in the day. Maybe he had made a speech where the big Latin words didn't go over. Who can tell?

That day he'd come into the room during his daily ritual. He asked me why I didn't walk up and down the hall as the doc in charge had advised. I explained to him that my doc hadn't given me any specific time to begin doing this, as long as it was done at some point. Really, I was still trying just to sit up in the chair without getting tired. All of a sudden he started screaming at me, saying I was slick, shrewd, trying to avoid doing what was ordered. What a performance he gave! I told him going down the hall would be difficult for me until I had gained more strength. The people would tire me.

"What people?" he screamed. Big question, mister. Knowing I had been all these years in the theatre, this man didn't realize I meant people would talk to me and I to them, thus making me exhausted. This was a hospital, not a theatre. My doc had said talking was the most tiring thing I could do. The nurse was upset. The lady scrubbing the floor was so upset that I think if he hadn't stopped harassing me she would have broken that mop over his head, which he wasn't using at that time. The nurse walked out of the room. What could she do? I was getting ready to sing out, weak as a kitten, and still he raved. It sounded like a barroom brawl. And by the time he finished, about twenty or thirty minutes later, I was a patient for sure.

Not long after the big scene, Doc came to visit, and this man is not easily fooled. He could sense his patient was pretty upset, and I told him I'd tell him what happened if he promised not to speak to anyone of the incident. He said he would consider it.

Perhaps the worst thing I could have done was to start talking about what had occurred. As the story grew, so did the emotions, and he could see it. Then Lou came in and again it was discussed. How this man had ripped! My nerves were gone. Later in the evening the situation got worse, and man, medicine, and machines went to work to save almost a disaster. Some of it I remember, some I don't. One thing I do recall passing through my mind, and, strange as it may seem, it's the one thing I've been running from all my life: that "pedestal" that fame puts you on, and which makes people react dishonestly to you. I was begging in my foggy mind, "Louis, get the ants off. The ants, those workers clamoring over each other, running over each other, picking up the crumbs, putting it in the holes, busy, busy, busy all the time." When you're buried up to your neck in honey (the syrup of others' dishonesty has been poured over you), the ants move in. I have a great respect for ants, but very little for people who imitate them, taking on the ant form. Take on their ambition and initiative, that's useful. Be as wise as they but don't become one, Human.

I learned many valuable things on that bed. So much agony came out that day with the young doctor. All the knots were untied. Thanks, Doc. You pushed me to greater understanding. I saw that spiritual leadership is the only real influence. Physical strength or brutal demand never pulled anyone anyplace.

When the fog lifted, they offered to let me go to another floor. It was all so disturbing. But I stayed. I'm sure many things were said to him. The next day that same young doctor walked back into my room again (without permission) and stood at the foot of my bed. Know what I did? I smiled at him. Why, I don't know. Actually, I think he was sick of himself.

This man was treating human beings and I kept praying he would be a better and more understanding person by the time he had his own practice. Yet the medical profession is the same as others, I guess. Some make good doctors like some make good shoe cobblers. A good shoe cobbler puts on the sole with soul and love. This doc was pulling off a soul. He had book learning and no compassion. Someday we'll meet again, and I do hope he is a credit to the great profession he has chosen.

The one thing that most humans don't like to recognize, unfortunately, is God. Would you believe it? People call themselves atheists and things, and I don't believe it. I think they really know there is something inside, that God is in all things we touch, that He is in each one of us. But they're afraid that if they should bring this thing out it would change them into something strange. I think that all of us reach a time when we know about ourselves—that great mastery of self. That's what I'm striving for.

There's a period of life when we swallow a knowledge of ourselves, and it becomes either good or sour inside. We can even start to get a certain bitterness that wears a person down in body. In the hospital I realized the mistake of that. I had a rebirth of an acceptance of people. I realized that I could accept people as they are.

One night I received a revelation. It must have been when I was at a low ebb and not much hope was held for body or soul. I can't remember it clearly at all, but I know now I must have been praying for true deliverance unto God. I do know that what happened then has made my life beautiful and full of understanding. I found myself writing down a prayer. When I was going through my papers and read this later, I wept at its beauty, and I hope you take these words to your hearts and keep them warm with love. I was praying for you, too, friends.

Dear God, speak to me tonight, give me a little more wisdom, more knowledge, more love and un-

derstanding for my fellow man. Cleanse me of all my misgivings and set me straight on the path. Direct my feet to the places where I can speak of You with great reverence. Open ears so they can hear of the great things that are here for us. Let us awaken to all the beauties of the earth, let the peace that passes all understanding reach out now to all mankind. We are in trouble, we are confused, we are bitter, going down deeper and deeper into the mire. Throw us a branch strong enough to pull us out. Our feet are stuck in the Clay of Hate, Deceit, and Malice. Soften the earth where we stand so we can loosen ourselves, teach us to smile again. Let me walk with and for Your cause alone, alone. OH! GOD I am listening every day. What is this thing I must do? If I'm not ready, speak directions in my ears, guide my feet, quicken my thoughts. Prepare me, dear Lord, prepare me. Help us to learn to help ourselves. We stand in our corners waiting for You. You are there—You are here—let us join with You.

The hills were ahead of me one day. From the hospital bed I could see the mountains and there came this beautiful thought. Yesterday I had been behind them, clawing at the rocks, trying to get back. How did I get back? I just got back, it's as simple as that. It will be better from now on —not just acceptance of many, but especially acceptance of one. You never find yourself until you face the truth.

14

---◆---

When I got out of the hospital I was wondering, "How will they receive me, the audiences?" But my first show was just a wonderful reception. There's no longer anymore the feeling of theatrical applause for me. The applause that I hear now says, "Welcome," or "We're glad to see you." That's another applause altogether. I think that whatever we feel comes out theatrically in our work. That's why if you take your troubles to the stage, it will show; the inner self will always tell the truth. Well, this opening after the hospital experience was one of the nights when everything is just molded within you and you feel it. A true performer never needs anyone to tell him when it was a good show. No one can tell you better than yourself. It's not egotistical; it's just a satisfaction that comes from within. There's a feeling of work well done that needs no explanation.

It was soon after this great reception that Robby, my ex-husband Jim's son, came to me unexpectedly and said that his grandma wanted to see me. (I told you I would get back to telling you about her.) We went out to this boy's house, and as he had explained, his grandmother was very weak. It was something like trouble with the arteries. She was in her late seventies.

We got there at eight-thirty and she was in bed. They had told her I was coming up to see her. Robby said, "I'll wake Grandma up and you can go in there, but wait." So I waited for just a second and then walked into the room. He snapped the light on. She was just lying there, all smiles. I went over and there was nothing to do but kneel down by the bed. This woman in her late seventies was the most gorgeous and beautiful woman I had ever seen. I don't mean just beautiful as an expression, I mean real facial beauty. At one time she really was known as one of the most beautiful women in Washington.

I knelt by the bed. And you know what she said to me? She said, "I didn't think you were coming." I hadn't seen this woman in fifteen years. But I remembered she was the one who had told me years ago that I should wear all East Indian colors, and I still do quite a bit, too. Regardless of the relationship there had been between her son and myself, when I met this woman from the very beginning there was something special.

Well, I was prepared for anything because they had told me her mind might wander. Three or four of her grandchildren were just standing around. I could feel that they were amazed, because there was no wandering in her conversation. They had told me that she didn't say much to them in a day, but we were talking and remembering everything.

After a little, we left her and went back into the living room and had coffee and hard-shell crabs and everything. Now it was about two-thirty in the morning, and Robby said, "I'll go and just tap Grandma, and if she's not too sleepy, you can wave goodbye." Well, we had been having this wonderful time of reunion with wonderful friends and now it was time to go. But I couldn't feel right about it because I couldn't leave my thoughts about that back room where Grandma was. All the time we were having the food, it was still she who was in my mind.

So he said, "I'll wake her up." I said," I bet she's not asleep." We walked into the room, and he went first to waken her. He was going to turn the light on, and I followed directly behind him. When I hit the door, he was just standing there with his mouth open. There was a mistiness in his eyes because already he had seen something. When I walked in the door I saw that this woman had gotten up out of the bed and was sitting in a chair and waiting and waiting for me to come back. Now, she usually did not get up out of her bed by herself; they carried her. She was up and she was sitting.

Well, her daughters and the three grandchilden came to see. You could feel that they were almost ready to cry. And we posed for pictures, and her grandson took some shots of us together. Her children were saying, "Has something happened to her? She hasn't been out of that bed by herself; she positively doesn't do it." While we were taking the pictures, I knelt down by the chair and we noticed that our hands are just alike. She had a beautiful manicure with nails as long as mine, just elegant hands.

Everybody was standing around there, real misty. I mean there was no idea that she's passing or anything; it was just that it was like a miracle. This whole thing came very close to me, so I turned to the old woman and I said, "Alma, I'm going to write a book." And then something happened which I can never forget. She straightened up in that chair, and she turned and pointed her finger at me, and she said, "You write that book. You *must* write it." To me that was really a command. Right away I started thinking of all the parts of my life which I could put in this book, and all of the things that I had learned which I wanted to put in there.

One by one I was reliving them all. I was standing on the corner in Newport News, a two-year-old child, saying, "Howdo, howdo." I was on the coal circuit playing rummy in the back room where the pool tables were. I was praying backstage at the Strand. Once again, I could hear the screaming for encores with the USO in Texas. All of it came right back.

I remembered the tattoo parlor and the Palladium and the crowds waiting outside the chapel when Louis and I were married. I remembered all of the rough times which you sometimes forget, and I remembered the joys.

Well now, I have followed the command as best I can. I am all warm from just putting down all of those little things that we can cherish in a life. And I'm putting it there for you, dear readers, with love from Pearl, with all the great love.

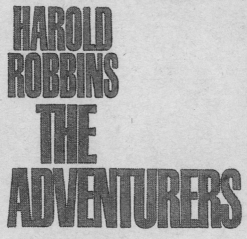

HAROLD ROBBINS
THE ADVENTURERS

12501/$1.25